HELP YOUR
LAWYER
WIN YOUR
CASE

HELP YOUR
LAWYER
WIN YOUR
CASE

Second Edition

J. Michael Hayes
Attorney at Law

SPHINX® PUBLISHING
A Division of Sourcebooks, Inc®
Naperville, IL • Clearwater, FL

Second edition, 1999
       Published by: **Sphinx® Publishing, A Division of Sourcebooks, Inc.®**

Sourcebooks Office	Sphinx Publishing Office
P.O. Box 4410	P.O. Box 25
Naperville, Illinois 60567-4410	Clearwater, Florida 33757
630-961-3900	727-587-0999
FAX: 630-961-2168	FAX: 727-586-5088

Interior Design and Production: Amy S. Hall and Edward A. Haman, Sourcebooks, Inc.®

This publication is designed to provide accurate and authoritative information in regard to the subject matter covered. It is sold with the understanding that the publisher is not engaged in rendering legal, accounting, or other professional service. If legal advice or other expert assistance is required, the services of a competent professional person should be sought.

From a Declaration of Principles Jointly Adopted by a Committee of the American Bar Association and a Committee of Publishers and Associations

This product is not a substitute for legal advice.

Disclaimer required by Texas statutes

Library of Congress Cataloging-in-Publication Data

Hayes, J. Michael.
      Help your lawyer win your case / J. Michael Hayes. -- 2nd ed.
            p.   cm.
      Includes index.
      ISBN 1-57248-103-X   (pbk.)
      1. Attorney and client--United States Popular works. I. Title.
KF311.Z9H39   1999
347.73 ' 504--dc21   99-32269
                                                                         CIP

Printed and bound in the United States of America.

LC Paperback — 10 9 8 7 6 5 4 3

CONTENTS

INTRODUCTION

I am a lawyer. However, this book was not written for lawyers. It was written for everyone who employs a lawyer to represent them in pursuing a claim, or defending against a claim, in court.

While lawyers may "win" cases, they rarely do so without the assistance of their clients. In fact, the assistance a client is able to give their lawyer may well make the difference between winning or losing in court.

If you employ a lawyer to represent you in court, there are a number of ways in which you can help the lawyer win your case. This book tells you what you can do to help and how to do it. By following the suggestions offered here, you can substantially increase your chances of success on your claim or defense. Moreover, by helping your lawyer in many of the ways suggested, you may significantly reduce the amount of legal fees and other costs you will pay in pursuing your case.

The suggestions contained in this book are applicable to claims and defenses in both state and federal courts. Many of the suggestions are also applicable to defending against criminal charges. This book is a complete, step-by-step guide to help you help your lawyer win your case.

When you employ a lawyer to pursue a claim or defense in court, you are making an investment of your time and money. As with any other investment, you owe it to yourself to do whatever you can to make that investment a profitable one and to reduce the cost of pursuing it as much as possible. This book will help you accomplish both objectives.

THE LEGAL PROCESS 1

This book deals with lawsuits brought in the court system in the United States. In order to help your lawyer win your case in a lawsuit, it will be helpful for you to have a basic understanding of our legal system.

TYPES OF LAWSUITS

Generally, lawsuits may be divided into two categories:

1. ***Criminal Cases.*** These are cases in which the government (through an agency, such as a federal or state prosecuting attorney's office) accuses a person (called the *defendant*) of committing a crime. The possible results for a losing defendant include imprisonment, a probationary term, a fine, or an order requiring the payment of restitution to a victim.

2. ***Civil Cases.*** These are cases in which one party (called the *plaintiff*) is suing another party (also called the *defendant*) for money or some other type of relief. The results for a losing plaintiff may include having to pay for the

defendant's attorney's fees and court costs (in addition to their own attorney's fees and court costs). The results for a losing defendant may include having to pay to the plaintiff money damages, or to give some other type of relief to the plaintiff; and having to pay for the plaintiff's attorney's fees and court costs (in addition to their own attorney's fees and court costs).

Within the category of civil cases, there are several subdivisions. The primary types of civil cases are:

☛ *Contract Cases.* These involve disputes arising out of a written or oral agreement between the parties and include actions for damages for breach of an express or implied contract, and actions to require a contract to be performed.

☛ *Tort Cases.* A tort is an injury to a person or property. Tort cases include actions for damages for negligence (such as automobile accidents, other accidents, professional malpractice, and defective products), assault and battery, false arrest, malicious prosecution, interference with an advantageous business relationship, fraud, libel, and slander.

☛ *Domestic Relations Cases.* These involve divorce and child custody disputes and include issues of alimony, child support, property division, and child custody and visitation.

☛ *Probate Cases.* These involve disputes concerning wills, the distribution of the estate of a deceased person, and claims of creditors against an estate.

☛ *Real Property Cases.* These involve disputes regarding land and include actions to stop a nuisance, to remove encroachments on land, to establish legal title to land, and to enforce or remove zoning and other restrictions on the use of land.

☛ *Statutory Actions.* These are cases based on rights created by statutes (laws). These include workers' compensation claims; copyright and patent infringement claims; and employment discrimination claims involving discharge or demotion because of age, sex, religion, national origin, or physical disability.

ALTERNATIVE DISPUTE RESOLUTION

There are two procedures that are sometimes available, either instead of going to court or before going to court. These are *mediation* and *arbitration,* in which claims are submitted to a third-party, outside of the court system, for resolution. Each of these procedures (together they are called *litigation alternatives* or *alternative dispute resolution*) will be briefly explained below, although a comprehensive discussion is beyond the scope of this book. Because of the variations in the availability and use of these procedures throughout the nation, you will need to discuss the specifics with your lawyer.

Mediation. In mediation, the role of the third-party (the *mediator*) is to listen to both sides of the case and try to help the parties reach a settlement. The mediator does not have the power to make a decision as to who wins, but is more of a neutral negotiator. Mediation sessions often involve the mediator meeting with each party separately and both parties together. The mediator's role is to facilitate a settlement by such things as identifying where the parties can agree, pointing out possible weak points in each party's case (to that party only), finding out what each party really wants, and suggesting possible settlement arrangements that will come as close as possible to meeting the goals of both parties. In some states, and in federal courts, even if you decide not to use either of these alternatives, the trial judge presiding over your case may order that the parties at least attempt to resolve the dispute by mediation before proceeding further in court.

Arbitration. In arbitration, the case is conducted like a trial, except that it is heard by an *arbitrator* (or two of more arbitrators) instead of by a judge or jury. The arbitrator may also encourage the parties to reach a settlement, but ultimately has the power to make a decision as to which party wins. In some states, arbitration may be required by either the law or the terms of a contract. For example, there may be a law in your state ordering that all medical malpractice claims must be submitted to arbitration before a lawsuit can be filed. Or you may be involved in a contract dispute, and the contract provides that all disputes will first be submitted to arbitration. In some cases, the arbitrator's decision is final (subject to appeal to an appellate court); and in other cases, a dissatisfied party may take the case to trial before a judge. Again, this may depend upon state law or the terms of a contract.

Use of these alternatives has become more common recently, primarily because they may reduce legal costs and can usually be completed in less time than required by litigation in court.

There are significant differences between these litigation alternatives and litigation, as well as significant differences between the alternative processes themselves. There are also significant advantages, and disadvantages, to using these alternatives as a substitute for litigation. These differences, advantages, and disadvantages are beyond the scope of this book. However, you should discuss them with your lawyer. If you and your lawyer decide to pursue either of these litigation alternatives, or mediation is ordered by the trial judge, most of the suggestions found in this book will be helpful. Those few suggestions which would not be helpful will be readily apparent once your lawyer has explained the alternative processes to you.

DEMAND LETTERS

The next chapter explains the trial process of our legal system. Sometimes, however, the trial process is avoided by a *demand letter*. This is a letter from the plaintiff's attorney to the defendant (or the defendant's attorney) advising of the nature of the plaintiff's claim, the amount of compensation or other form of relief being sought, and that a lawsuit will be filed unless the claim can be resolved. A demand letter usually gives the defendant (or the defendant's attorney) a deadline in which to respond and states that a lawsuit will be filed after this date if the response is not received in time.

The purpose of a demand letter is to attempt to settle the claim as quickly and inexpensively as possible. If you are a potential plaintiff, whether your attorney sends a demand letter and its contents, will depend on the circumstances of your particular case and on your lawyer's advice. If you are a potential defendant, how you will respond to a demand letter will depend on the circumstances of your particular defense (or defenses) to the plaintiff's claim, and on the advice of your lawyer.

Whether you are a potential plaintiff or a potential defendant, the suggestions contained in chapter 4 will help you to help your lawyer in dealing with a demand letter.

What Is Winning?

One thing you will need to consider, especially after you have met with your attorney and as your case progresses, is what it means to *win* a case. In some cases, the best way to win your case is either not to pursue it in the first place, or to pursue it only to a limited extent in order to obtain a reasonable compromise or settlement. Winning your case means doing what is best for you. Whether or not the pursuit of your claim or defense to its conclusion in litigation is best for you depends on several factors. In litigation, as in anything else, you owe it to yourself to consider these factors in determining what course of action is in your best interest.

In deciding whether to pursue your claim or defense, or deciding to what extent you wish to pursue it, you should consider the following factors:

☛ What are my anticipated fees and costs in pursuing my case?

☛ To what extent, if any, will I have the right to seek reimbursement for my anticipated fees and costs from my opponent if I am successful?

☛ What are my chances of success on my claim or defense?

☛ What is my anticipated exposure if I am successful in my case? (The concept of *exposure* is discussed more in the section on "What to Ask Your Lawyer" in chapter 4.)

☛ What is my anticipated exposure if I am unsuccessful?

☛ If I am successful on my claim or defense, and I am legally entitled to be reimbursed for my losses (that is, damages, attorney's fees, and costs) from my opponent, will I be able to collect those losses from my opponent?

In a hypothetical, ideal situation, if you were able to obtain reliable answers to each of the above questions, the decision as to whether to proceed further with your claim or defense would be an easy one. Unfortunately, litigation is an art, not a science, and in most cases it will not be possible for you to obtain reliable, clear-cut answers to these questions. This is so for a number of reasons, and it would serve no useful purpose to discuss them in detail here. However, the fact that you cannot hope to obtain reliable, clear-cut answers to these questions does not mean that it is useless to ask them, or that you cannot benefit from answering them at least to a limited extent. A few examples will illustrate the point:

Example No. 1: You have a claim for $25,000. However, in pursuing your claim, you will be obligated to pay approximately $15,000 in fees and costs, for which you will not be reimbursed even if you are successful. You may well decide such a claim is not worth pursuing.

Example No. 2: Your claim is for $25,000. However, in your lawyer's opinion, your chances for success are fifty percent or less. You may decide it is not worth pursuing the claim.

Example No. 3: You have a claim for $25,000. However, even if you are successful, you have no clear indication that a judgment in your favor would be collectible from your opponent. Again, you may decide it is not worth pursuing the claim.

Obviously, there are a number of variations of the above examples which can be applicable in your particular case and which may lead you to conclude that it is not in your best interest to pursue your claim or defense, or that you should pursue it only to the extent of attempting to reach a compromise or settlement.

In view of the above considerations, the best you can accomplish may be to "make the best of a bad situation." Ask your lawyer these questions, and make your decision based on the best estimates to these questions the lawyer can provide. Before making your decision, ask your lawyer for advice.

A final suggestion: Before deciding whether to pursue your case in court, discuss with your lawyer the possibility of using the alternative dispute resolution procedures explained above.

THE TRIAL PROCESS 2

Before discussing the ways in which you can help your lawyer win your case, you should be aware of certain basic facts concerning the trial process and how it works.

If a person (whether an individual, partnership, corporation, or some other form of artificial body) has suffered a financial, physical, or emotional loss because of an act, or a failure to act, by another person; they may have a right to bring a legal action in a court seeking repayment, reimbursement, or other compensation for that loss. They (as a *plaintiff*) will begin that process by filing a *complaint* or *statement of claim*, setting forth their claim, in an appropriate court. The other party (the *defendant*) will file a response, usually called an *answer* or an *answer and defenses*, in which they will state their position as to why they are not legally responsible for the loss.

In addition to filing an answer, the defendant may have a claim against the plaintiff, either based on the transaction about which they are being sued or some other transaction. If so, the defendant may file that claim, usually called a *counterclaim*.

If there are several defendants in the action, and one or more of them believe that the loss the plaintiff may have suffered was caused by another defendant, they may assert that claim, usually called a *cross-claim.*

Finally, if a defendant believes that, while the plaintiff may have suffered a loss, that loss was caused by a third-party who is not presently a defendant in the action, they may assert that claim, usually called a *third-party claim.*

Prior to the filing of an answer, there may be several motions filed by the defendant which could take weeks or even months to resolve. One type is a *motion to dismiss,* which argues that the complaint is not legally sufficient. If a defendant wins a motion to dismiss, the plaintiff is usually given additional time to file a new complaint. A new motion to dismiss may be filed, or the case may move forward on the filing of an answer.

Another is a *motion for a more definite statement* (sometimes called a *motion for bill of particulars*), which argues that the complaint is too vague or unclear. If such a motion is granted, the judge orders the plaintiff to file an additional paper to clarify what is in the complaint.

If you are a defendant, the filing of such motions may be necessary to narrow or clarify the issues to be resolved. You will then be better prepared to later defeat the claim of the plaintiff or to eliminate, early in the lawsuit, a claim which is not legally supportable. This will save you time and money by not having to put up an unnecessary defense.

If you are a plaintiff, the filing of such motions and the delay they will cause, can be frustrating. Indeed, many defendants know that the filing of legally permissible motions may frustrate and discourage the plaintiff. However, keep in mind that delays are unavoidable in lawsuits. Such motions may even benefit you as the plaintiff, either because they provide advance notice of possible problems with your case (which your lawyer may be able to correct or overcome before it is too late); or because they alert your lawyer to possible defenses to your claim at an early stage (again, allowing you and your attorney to more effectively counter them). The point is that you should not be surprised if such motions are filed, you should be mentally prepared for delays, and you should not be discouraged or unduly frustrated by them.

After an answer is filed, there may also be motions filed, such as a *motion for summary judgment*, or *motion for judgment on the pleadings*. In essence, these motions argue that even if what the other party claims is true, they are not legally entitled to judgment in their favor. If these motions are granted, that usually ends the case unless the losing side appeals.

If a possibility of filing such motions arises in your case, your attorney should discuss with you the advantages and disadvantages of filing them. Such motions always delay the case, and they may have little or no likelihood of improving the ultimate outcome of the case.

For example, while there may be a technical reason for dismissal of a complaint, the granting of a motion to dismiss may only result in the filing of a revised complaint (which may even benefit the legal position of the plaintiff).

Once a complaint and an answer (and any counterclaims, cross-claims, or third-party claims) have been filed, the lawyers for the parties begin the process of *pre-trial discovery*. This process simply means that the lawyers for all sides will use legally recognized methods to learn the details of all parties' positions, both legally and factually.

After pre-trial discovery has been completed, the matter will be scheduled for trial. At trial, the lawyers for the plaintiff and the defendant (and for other parties, if any) will present *evidence* in support of their positions in the form of *testimony* from witnesses and documents, if any.

After the presentation of evidence, the fact-finder, which may be either a judge or a jury, will decide what the facts are, apply the law to those facts, and issue (*render*) a *verdict* or *judgment*. If either of the parties does not agree with that verdict or judgment, usually it can be reviewed and perhaps changed, by another court through the *appellate* process. The complete trial and appellate process is sometimes referred to as *litigation* or, in a specific case, as *the litigation*.

Of course, this brief summary is over-simplified. Each of these stages or events in the trial and appellate process can involve complicated questions of law. However, you need not concern yourself with, or even understand, those legal questions in order to help your lawyer win your case. You need only know what, specifically, you can do to help your lawyer win.

Generally, there are five areas in litigation in which you can help your lawyer win your case:

1. Identifying the facts which may have a bearing on your claim or defense.

2. Identifying, and locating, witnesses who may be helpful to your case.

3. Identifying, and locating, documents or writings which may be helpful to your case.

4. Avoiding unnecessary inconsistencies in presenting your position in the litigation.

5. Identifying factually incorrect or inconsistent positions in your opponent's case.

Each of these areas of assistance, together with specific suggestions regarding each area, will be discussed in detail in this book. Before beginning that discussion, the following general comments should be kept in mind throughout your reading of this book:

☞ The suggestions offered here are general ones, applicable to all types of cases which are to be resolved in court, regardless of the specific type or nature of the claim or defense involved. However, each case in litigation is different. Your lawyer will no doubt have additional suggestions, tailored to your particular case, as to how you can assist in the trial and appellate process. By all means, ask for, and follow, those suggestions.

☞ Many of the suggestions which follow will not only assist you in helping your lawyer win your case, but may also result in a reduction of your legal fees. These suggestions will have that result where the amount of those fees will be determined, at least in part, by the amount of time your lawyer spends on your case. These suggestions may reduce fees by reducing the amount of time your lawyer will be required to spend on your case. In some cases, either a third-party (such as your insurance company) will pay your lawyer, or you will be obligated to pay for your lawyer's services at a fixed amount regardless of how much time your lawyer spends on the case. In either of these two situations, these suggestions will not result in a financial savings to you. However, following these particular suggestions (like all of the other suggestions found in this book) will nevertheless be of benefit to you, since they will increase your chances of success.

☞ Some of the suggestions which follow concern ways in which you may be able to help your lawyer perform a particular task or function which is the primary responsibility of the lawyer. For example, it is suggested that you can assist your lawyer in determining the scope of questions to be asked of witnesses, locating inconsistencies in the testimony of your opponent and your opponent's witnesses, and identifying important factual matters which might be brought to the attention of the fact-finder. Of course, these suggestions, and several others of a similar nature, concern a task which will be performed by your lawyer in the normal course of his or her representation of you. Lawyers are trained, and especially qualified, to perform these tasks. Moreover, a particular lawyer may delegate the performance of some of these tasks to paralegal personnel. "Paralegal" personnel are persons who are not licensed to practice law, but have been trained to assist lawyers in various legal matters. If paralegal personnel are used in your case, usually you will be charged for their time. Since these suggestions concern matters which your lawyer (or paralegal personnel) will already be performing on your behalf, you might ask, "Why should I offer to assist in the performance of these tasks?" There are several reasons:

- Your assistance may act as a safe-guard in assuring that no matter important to your case is overlooked. Trials, and related proceedings, are frequently fast-paced, often requiring your lawyer to speak or act within a very limited time-span, and, under such pressures, it may well be that "two heads are better than one."

- Your assistance may reduce the time spent by your lawyer (or paralegal) in performing certain tasks, thereby perhaps reducing your legal (or paralegal) fees.

- Many of the suggestions concern areas where the participation of two persons, rather than one, will be helpful, and your lawyer has no one else to assist.

Of course, in your particular case, your lawyer may not need your assistance in performing any one or more of these particular tasks, and would prefer to perform them without your assistance. If your lawyer has such a preference, abide by that preference.

Hiring a Lawyer 3

In the event you do not yet have a lawyer, or are thinking about getting a new lawyer, the following suggestions are offered about the important preliminary process of selecting an attorney to represent you.

First, you should make appointments with two or three attorneys, then decide if you want to hire one of them.

FINDING LAWYERS

There are several ways to begin the process:

- ☞ Ask a friend. A common, and frequently the best, way to find a lawyer is to ask someone you know to recommend one to you. This is especially helpful if the lawyer represented your friend in a similar type of legal matter.

- ☞ Lawyer Referral Service. You can find a referral service by looking in the Yellow Pages phone directory under "Attorney Referral Services" or "Attorneys." This is a service, usually operated by a bar association, which is designed to match a client with an attorney handling cases in the area of law the client needs. The referral service does not guarantee the quality of work, nor the level of experience or ability of the attorney. Finding a lawyer this way will at least connect you with one who is interested in the area of law concerning your type of case.

☛ Yellow Pages. Check under the heading for "Attorneys" in the Yellow Pages phone directory. Many of the lawyers and law firms will place display ads here indicating their areas of practice and educational back grounds.

☛ Ask another lawyer. If you have used the services of an attorney in the past for some other matter (for example, a real estate closing, traffic ticket or a will), you may want to call and ask if he or she could refer you to an attorney whose ability in the area of your problem is respected.

EVALUATING A LAWYER

From your search you should select three to five lawyers worthy of further consideration. Your first step will be to call each attorney's office, *briefly* explain the type of problem you have, and ask the following questions:

☛ Does the attorney (or firm) handle this type of matter?

☛ How much is an initial consultation? (It may be free or for a minimal cost.)

☛ How soon can you get an appointment?

If you like the answers you get, ask if you can speak to the attorney. Some offices will permit this, but others will require you to make an appointment. Make the appointment if that is what is required. Once you get in contact with the attorney (either on the phone or at the appointment), ask the following questions:

- ☞ How much will it cost? (Don't expect a definite answer, but a range and the variables should be discussed.)
- ☞ How will the fee be paid?
- ☞ How long has the attorney been in practice?
- ☞ How long has the attorney been in practice in your state?
- ☞ Has the attorney handled similar matters previously?

If you get acceptable answers, it's time to ask yourself the following questions about the lawyer:

- ☞ Do you feel comfortable talking to the lawyer?
- ☞ Is the lawyer friendly toward you?
- ☞ Does the lawyer seem confident in himself or herself?
- ☞ Does the lawyer seem to be straight-forward with you, and able to explain things so you understand?

If you get satisfactory answers to all of these questions, you probably have a lawyer with whom you'll be able to work. Most clients are happiest with an attorney with whom they feel comfortable.

WORKING WITH A LAWYER

In general, you will work best with your attorney if you keep an open, honest, and friendly attitude. You should also consider the following suggestions.

Ask questions. If you want to know something or if you don't understand something, ask your attorney. If you don't understand the answer, tell your attorney and ask him or her to explain it again. There are many points of law that many lawyers don't fully understand, so you shouldn't be embarrassed to ask questions. Many people who say they had a bad experience with a lawyer either didn't ask enough questions, or had a lawyer who wouldn't take the time to explain things to them. It may be time to look for a new lawyer if your lawyer won't take the time to explain what he's doing.

Give your lawyer complete information. Anything you tell your attorney is confidential (this is the "attorney-client privilege"). An attorney can lose his license to practice if he reveals information without your permission. So don't hold back. Tell your lawyer everything, even if it doesn't seem important to you. There are many things which seem unimportant to a non-attorney, but can change the outcome of a case. Also, don't hold something back because you are afraid it will hurt your case. It will definitely hurt your case if your lawyer doesn't find out about it until he hears it in court from your opponent's attorney! But if he knows in advance, he can plan to eliminate or reduce the damage.

Accept reality. Listen to what your lawyer tells you about the law and the system. It will do you no good to argue because the law or the system doesn't work the way you think it should. For example, if your lawyer tells you that the judge can't hear your case for two weeks, don't try demanding that he set a hearing tomorrow. By refusing to accept reality, you are only setting yourself up for disappointment. And remember: It's not your attorney's fault that the system isn't perfect, or that the law doesn't say what you'd like it to say.

Be patient. This applies to being patient with the system (which is often slow as discussed earlier), as well as with your attorney. Don't expect your lawyer to return your phone call within the hour. She may not even be able to return it the same day. Most lawyers are very busy and over-worked. It is rare that an attorney can maintain a full case load and still make each client feel as if he is the only client.

Talk to the secretary. Your lawyer's secretary can be a valuable source of information. So be friendly and get to know him. Often, he will be able to answer your questions and you won't get a bill for the time you talk to him.

Let your attorney deal with your opponent. It is your lawyer's job to communicate with your opponent, or with your opponent's lawyer. Let your lawyer do this. Many lawyers have had clients lose or damage their cases when the client decides to say or do something on their own.

Be on time. This applies to appointments with your lawyer and to court hearings.

Keeping your case moving. Many lawyers operate on the old principle of "The squeaking wheel gets the oil." Work on a case tends to get put off until a deadline is near, an emergency develops, or the client calls. There is a reason for this. After many years of education (and the expense of that education), lawyers hope to earn the income due a professional. This is difficult with a great many attorneys competing for clients, and the high cost of office overhead. Many lawyers find it necessary to take a large number of cases in order to make an acceptable living. That is why many attorneys work sixty-five hours a week or more. Your task is to become a squeaking wheel that doesn't squeak too much. Whenever you talk to your lawyer, ask the following questions:

- ☛ What is the next step?
- ☛ When do you expect it to be done?
- ☛ When should I talk to you next?

If you don't hear from the lawyer when you expect, call him the following day. Don't remind him that he didn't call—just ask how things are going.

How to save money. Of course, you don't want to spend unnecessary money for an attorney. Here are a few things you can do to avoid excess legal fees:

- ☛ Don't make unnecessary phone calls to your lawyer.
- ☛ Give information to the secretary when possible.
- ☛ Direct your question to the secretary first. She'll refer you to the attorney if she can't answer it.
- ☛ Plan your phone calls so you can get to the point and take less of your attorney's time.
- ☛ Do some of the "leg work" yourself. Pick up and deliver papers yourself, for example. Ask your attorney what you can do to assist with your case.
- ☛ Be prepared for appointments. Have all related papers with you, plan your visit to get to the point, and make an outline of what you want to discuss and what questions you want to ask.

Pay your attorney bill when it's due. No client gets prompt attention like a client who pays his lawyer on time. However, you are entitled to an itemized bill, showing what the attorney did and how much time it took. If you pay an advance (or "retainer," which is a sum of money to be applied to the ultimate fee to be arrived at later) to the lawyer, make certain you understand what services the lawyer will be performing for that advance. If you will be paying a flat fee for the lawyer's services, again, make certain you understand what services will be included in the fee.

Discharging your lawyer. If you find that you can no longer work with your lawyer, you may, or course, discharge him or her. You will need to send your lawyer a letter stating that you no longer desire his or her services, and are discharging him or her from your case. Also state that you will be coming by his or her office to pick up your file. The attorney does not have to give you his or her own notes or other work in progress, but he or she must give you the essential contents of your file (such as copies of papers already filed or prepared and billed for, and any documents you provided).

Usually, your initial meeting with a lawyer will be for the purpose of making the lawyer aware of the facts important to your claim or defense, and deciding whether the lawyer will represent you.

Assuming you have already decided to employ the lawyer to represent you, the objectives you wish to accomplish at the initial meeting will be three-fold:

1. Making certain the lawyer has the necessary information to evaluate and present your claim or defense

2. Persuading the lawyer to represent you

3. Arriving at an agreement with regard to attorneys' fees and court costs which you will, or may be, obligated to pay in pursuing your claim or defense

THE INITIAL 4
MEETING WITH
YOUR LAWYER

IMPORTANCE OF THE MEETING

Your initial meeting with the lawyer is extremely important, for several reasons.

First, the initial meeting is your first opportunity to make the lawyer aware of all of the facts which may have a bearing on your claim or defense. Without these facts, your lawyer cannot fully or accurately advise you of the merit, or lack of merit, of your claim or defense. As discussed in more detail later, this advice is important to you in determining whether you wish to pursue your claim or defense.

Second, assuming your claim or defense does have merit, this is your first opportunity to provide your lawyer with the information legally necessary to pursue it successfully. The information you provide at this meeting may well "set the stage" for much of the legal work which the lawyer will perform on your behalf from that point forward. Consequently, the information you provide, and the manner in which you provide it, can have a decisive impact on your chances for success. Moreover, it is to your advantage to provide your lawyer with this information as soon as possible. A delay in providing that information can result in a delay in arriving at a successful conclusion, as well as increase your legal fees. And, in some cases, it may be necessary to take immediate legal action in order to protect your interest. A delay in providing the facts to your lawyer may result in your losing certain legal rights.

Third, the initial meeting will provide you with an opportunity to learn the potential costs (in legal fees and court costs) which may be involved. Frequently, the lawyer may not be in a position at this meeting to provide you with "hard and fast" information on this subject, for a simple reason: the lawyer may have no reliable means of knowing the extent of litigation that may be required in your case. However, frequently the lawyer can provide you with some information on the subject. This information is important to you, since it may have a bearing on whether you wish to pursue your claim or defense.

Finally, at this meeting, the lawyer will gain his or her first impression of you. That impression is important, since it may have an impact on whether the lawyer agrees to represent you. If the impression you give at the meeting is that of a person who is disorganized, uncommunicative, a rambling speaker, or less than candid and straight-forward, the lawyer may be reluctant to represent you. On the other hand, if you give the impression of being a person who is organized, communicative, direct and sincere, and candid, the lawyer will be much more likely to undertake your representation, no matter how difficult your claim or defense may be.

PREPARING FOR THE MEETING

By far, the most effective and helpful assistance you can give your lawyer at the initial meeting lies in providing all information in your possession which is, or may be, important to winning your case. No matter what the nature of your claim or defense, you possess information without which your lawyer cannot successfully pursue your case. Indeed, frequently it is the information you possess which is crucial to winning your case. Consequently, it is to your advantage to assure that you provide your lawyer with that information, as soon as possible and in the most effective manner possible. As a result, it is to your advantage to adequately prepare for the initial meeting with your lawyer.

How do you adequately prepare for the meeting? By identifying and organizing the information you possess which is important, or may be important, to your case. Obviously, in order to do so, you must be aware of the types of information you possess which will be helpful to your lawyer. A determination of what information might be helpful depends on a variety of factors, including the legal nature of your claim or defense, the particular law which is applicable to such a claim or defense, and the particular facts of your case.

Your lawyer is trained in the method of obtaining this information from you by asking you the right questions at the initial meeting. However, you can assist your lawyer in that process by anticipating those questions, and at least preliminarily, preparing to answer them before the meeting. That preparation will assure that, at the meeting, you provide ***all*** of the information in your possession which may be important to your case, as well as reduce the amount of time necessary for the meeting, thereby possibly reducing the amount of legal fees involved.

In preparing for the initial meeting, you should take adequate time to analyze your claim or defense and identify and organize the information in your possession regarding the case. In doing so, and if time permits, prepare a "written narrative" of the information you have identified in your preparation for the initial meeting with your lawyer. Such a narrative can take the form of an outline of the information you will be providing your lawyer at the meeting. That outline will assist you in making a more effective presentation of the information in your possession to your lawyer at the meeting.

In addition, it may reduce the time necessary for the meeting, which, in some cases, may reduce your legal fees. Be prepared to provide your lawyer with a copy of the narrative at the meeting, since reference to it by the lawyer may assist in their understanding of the information you are providing. Of course, retain either the original or a copy for yourself, for future reference. Throughout the course of the litigation, you may wish to add additional points or information which come to light, as a reference for making certain you provide any such information to your lawyer.

Before preparing a written narrative, however, ask your lawyer if you should prepare one, and, if so, in what form it should be prepared. If you do prepare one, make a notation on it that it is "attorney-client privileged" or words of like effect. Indeed, from this point forward, include such a notation on any written communication you have with your lawyer. Whether you prepare such a written narrative or not, you should be prepared to provide your lawyer with the following information (use the "Witness" and "Documents" forms in appendix B to help you):

☛ The date, time and place of each event or occurrence which concerns, bears on, or is connected with your claim or defense.

☛ To the best of your recollection, exactly what happened at any such event or occurrence. In presenting the substance of oral conversations, as best you can, relate the exact language used, in the order it was used; avoid paraphrasing. The language used, and it's sequence, may have legal significance.

☛ The names and current addresses of all persons who were present at any such event or occurrence.

☛ The names and current addresses of all persons with whom you have discussed any such event or occurrence.

☛ The names and current addresses of all persons who have discussed (or who may have discussed) any such event or occurrence with your opponent.

☛ A description of any writing prepared by you which refers to, or is connected with, any such event or occurrence, together with a description of its contents and its present location.

☛ A description of any writing prepared by your opponent which refers to, or is connected with, any such event or occurrence, together with a description of its contents and its present location.

☛ A description of any writing prepared by someone other than yourself or your opponent which refers to, or is connected with, any such event or occurrence, together with a description of its contents and its present location.

☛ The names and current addresses of any persons not included in the above categories, who have, or may have, knowledge or information concerning any such event or occurrence.

☛ A description of any other writing not included in the above categories, which refers to or is connected with any such event or occurrence, together with a description of its contents and its present location.

☛ The names and current addresses of all persons with whom you are acquainted, and who would, or might, be willing to testify in court that they are familiar with your general reputation in the community for truthfulness and honesty; and that your reputation is "good," "excellent," etc., together with a brief description of the nature of your relationship with them, their background, and the period of time in which you have been acquainted.

☛ The names and current addresses of all persons with whom your opponent is acquainted, and who would, or might, be willing to testify in court that they are familiar with the general reputation of your opponent in the community for truthfulness and honesty; and that his reputation is "bad," "not good," etc., together with a brief description of the nature of your opponent's relationship with them, their background, and the period of time in which they have been acquainted.

☛ A description of any photograph or videotape which portrays or is connected with any such event or occurrence, together with a description of what is portrayed and its present location.

☛ A description of any audiotape which refers to or is connected with any such event or occurrence, together with a description of its contents and its present location.

☛ If you are pursuing a claim for reimbursement or payment of monies due you, unrelated to physical or emotional injuries, you will wish to identify the specific amount(s) involved, together with the names and current addresses of any persons who have knowledge or information concerning the amount(s) claimed. You will also wish to identify any writing which refers to or is connected with the amount(s) involved, together with its present location.

☛ If you are pursuing a claim involving physical or emotional injuries, you will wish to identify the specific nature of those injuries, together with the names and current addresses of all persons who have, or may have, knowledge or information concerning those injuries. You will also want to provide a detailed and complete past medical history, including identification of all treating physicians or other healthcare providers, hospitalizations, insurance policies, insurance claims, and insurance payments. You should also provide any medical reports, medical bills, and any other related documents in your possession. If you have any such items, review them for accuracy. If you find them to be inaccurate in any way, be prepared to point out to your lawyer how they are inaccurate.

☛ The names and current addresses of any persons whom you know or suspect will dispute your version of the important facts, or will dispute the version of the important facts given by a witness who will support your claim or defense.

In most instances, the above information should be adequate, at least preliminarily, to acquaint your lawyer at the initial meeting with the basic knowledge and information in your possession which may be important to your case. Depending on the responses you make to some of the categories mentioned above, additional information should be provided. For example:

☛ If you have discussed any event or occurrence connected with your claim or defense with other persons, you should provide the lawyer with the time, date, and place of the discussion, together with a description of the contents of the discussion, and the names and current addresses of all persons who were present. The same is applicable to discussions your opponent may have had with other persons regarding any such event or occurrence.

☛ If your claim or defense concerns technical matters of any kind, or matters which may require some form of specialized knowledge, you will wish to provide your lawyer with:

- The names and current addresses of any persons who have, or may have, specialized knowledge concerning those matters.

- A description of any writing which refers to or is connected with any such technical matters or specialized knowledge; for example, textbooks, scholarly writings, treatises, or other publications in the field, together with their location or how they can be obtained by the lawyer.

☛ Of course, any writings, photographs, videotapes, or audio tapes you have identified in your responses to any of the above categories which are in your possession should be presented to your lawyer at the initial meeting. If any of these items are not currently in your possession, but you can obtain them prior to the initial meeting, do so.

☛ In some cases, you may have information concerning your opponent's involvement with third-parties which may have a bearing on your claim or defense. For example, you may have a claim against your opponent because of a defective product, and you are aware of other legal claims, pending lawsuits, etc., concerning the same or a similar product. If so, you should provide that information to your lawyer. Similarly, your claim or defense may be based on some form of fraud, deceit, or misrepresentation practiced by your opponent, which may have resulted in other legal claims, lawsuits, etc. If so, provide that information to your lawyer as well.

☞ If your claim or defense has received any media coverage (either print or television), you should make your lawyer aware of that fact, and provide any clippings, transcripts, audio or video tapes, etc. Similarly, if there has been media coverage concerning the subject matter of your claim or defense, for example, pending legal claims or lawsuits filed by third-parties, provide the details to your lawyer.

☞ If you know, or have reason to believe, that any of the discussions or conversations you have identified in your responses to any of the above categories have been electronically recorded (either by audio or video recording) without your consent, make your lawyer aware of that fact, and provide any tapes or transcripts of such conversations you may have in your possession, or the location of any such tapes or transcripts in the possession of third-parties.

☞ If you (or your opponent) have a prior criminal record, the details should be furnished to your lawyer. Similarly, if any important potential witness on your behalf, or on behalf of your opponent, has a prior criminal record, that information should be disclosed.

☞ If you have been a party to, or a witness at, any other prior or pending litigation, the details should be provided to your lawyer.

☞ If you have made oral or written statements which are, or could be argued to be, inconsistent with facts you will be bringing to the attention of your lawyer, be prepared to identify those statements, and to offer any appropriate explanation for the inconsistency. For example, you may have made a statement which has been taken out of context, or you may have made a statement without having had the benefit of additional facts. And, in some cases, a statement may have been attributed to you which you did not make.

In providing the names and location of all potential witnesses who may be important, keep in mind that, generally, there are two types of "witnesses":

1. A person who can, or might, establish or support an important fact in your case; and

2. A person who can, or might, establish or support any fact important in your opponent's case.

It is important to remember that there are two types of "supporting" witnesses:

1. A person who has **direct** knowledge of one or more of the facts important to your case (or that of your opponent). This is knowledge which was obtained at the time involved, i.e., a direct participant in the events; and

2. A person who has **indirect** knowledge of one or more of the facts important to your case (or that of your opponent). This is knowledge which was obtained through conversation, or some other form of communication (e.g., correspondence), with one or more of the direct participants. For example, after the important events, you may have had a conversation with a third person, who has no first-hand knowledge of the events, in which you told that person your version of the events. If, at trial, your opponent

attempts to attack your version of those events, i.e., attempts to attack your "credibility," your lawyer may be permitted to call such a person as a witness to show that the version of the events which you have testified to at trial is consistent with the version which you previously communicated to this other person, thereby supporting your credibility. Similarly, if you intend to attempt to question the credibility of your opponent at trial, and you are aware of the fact that, on a prior occasion, your opponent told a third-party a version of the important events which is clearly different from that version which your opponent is offering at trial, your lawyer may be able to call that person as a witness to show that inconsistency, thereby calling into question the credibility of your opponent.

There may also be a third type of supporting witness: an *expert* witness. An expert witness is merely a person who, because of special education, training or experience, has special knowledge concerning a subject—knowledge which the average person (or juror) may not have. In some instances, such experts are allowed to testify at trial for the purpose of assisting the jury (or a judge) in understanding the facts.

Finally, where credibility of witnesses is important, a fourth type of witness may be used: a *character* witness. A character witness is simply a person who has known you for a significant period of time, has discussed your reputation for truthfulness with other persons in the community, and can state an opinion as to whether your general reputation in the community for truthfulness is good or bad.

If your lawyer believes it is possible that your truthfulness will be attacked by your opponent, he or she might wish to offer such witnesses at trial to increase your believability with the judge or jury. (Similarly, in some instances, your lawyer may wish to offer "negative" character witnesses at trial. Negative character witnesses are persons who, because of their familiarity with your opponent, can state an opinion that your opponent's reputation for truthfulness is bad.)

Generally, such opinion testimony is not allowed at trial unless you (or your opponent) first testifies at trial, and an issue of credibility has been raised regarding that testimony. If such testimony is allowed at trial, it is not binding on the fact-finder and can be either accepted or rejected at the sole discretion of the fact-finder. If you have reason to believe that there may be a dispute between you and your opponent on any important issue of fact, and you know potential witnesses who would qualify as character witnesses on your behalf, or who might qualify as negative character witnesses, provide the names and addresses of those persons to your lawyer.

In identifying for your lawyer all witnesses or potential witnesses, you will wish to include any persons who fall within one or more of the above categories of witnesses. After you have identified all witnesses and potential witnesses, your lawyer will either interview or *depose* (i.e., take a formal statement from) such witnesses to determine whether they do, in fact, have information which may be important.

In identifying these witnesses for your lawyer, provide accurate addresses, telephone numbers, etc., for the witnesses, together with any knowledge you may have concerning their travel or future plans for residence; and whether any of them suffer from any serious medical condition. If an important witness will be unavailable to testify at trial, either because of a change in residence or a health problem, your lawyer may wish to perpetuate (obtain in usable form for trial) their testimony by taking their deposition for use at trial. Keep your lawyer currently advised on these subjects as the case progresses.

As noted above, you should provide your lawyer with any writings or other physical objects having a bearing on your claim or defense. If you will be presenting writings or objects at that meeting, and they are voluminous or more than a few, prepare an *inventory* or list of the items being presented with (if appropriate) a brief description of each item for use by the lawyer. Retain a copy for yourself.

FRANKNESS AND CANDOR

Before more fully addressing the subject of the initial meeting with your lawyer, a word about frankness and candor. In almost all cases, there are, at least arguably, two sides: yours and your opponent's. The simple fact is that your lawyer cannot effectively represent you unless you have made a full, complete, frank, and candid disclosure of **all** of the facts which may be important to your claim or defense. If your lawyer is ignorant of those facts, he or she will not be able to advise you effectively or present your case successfully. To the contrary, your lawyer may well unintentionally give advice, or proceed in a manner, which is damaging to your claim or defense.

Keep in mind that lawyers do not "judge" the facts or you; they present the important facts to an ultimate fact-finder (whether it is a judge or a jury) and point out the errors in your opponent's position. Many people believe that, if they tell their lawyer the truth, the lawyer may be reluctant to represent them or may not represent them. This is untrue. There may well be weaknesses to your claim or defense; however, that fact will not deter a good lawyer from representing you. After all, that is the very business of "lawyering." Moreover, keep in mind that what you believe may be a weakness in your claim or defense may not be a weakness after all. Or, if it is, it may be either unimportant or a weakness which your lawyer may be able to easily explain away in your favor. The point is, if your lawyer is not aware of the facts, you cannot expect he or she to address them effectively.

Even if there are weaknesses to your claim or defense, no useful purpose is served by failing to disclose them to your lawyer. To the contrary, if such weaknesses exist, it may be in your best interests not to pursue your claim or defense at all because of the costs involved. From your standpoint, if your claim or defense is not legally and factually supportable, you are much better off knowing that fact as soon as possible, so as to avoid "throwing good money after bad."

STATING THE FACTS

With the above points in mind, at the initial meeting with your lawyer, you should:

☞ When appropriate and applicable, provide the information you have identified and gathered in your preparation for the meeting.

☞ Provide a copy of your written narrative (or, if you have not prepared one, offer to do so).

☞ Present the important facts clearly and concisely, and, when discussing events, discuss them in the order in which they occurred (that is, chronologically).

☞ Avoid referring to facts which are obviously not important. For example, if the issue is an increase in child support, you should not give a long history of all of your visitation or custody problems.

☞ Be careful to separate fact from guesses. (This is not to say that you should not inform the lawyer of matters which are based on speculation or guesswork; however, you should make it clear when you do so.)

☞ Leave your emotions at home. If the facts important to your claim or defense show that your opponent has taken unfair advantage of you, or seriously harmed you, those facts speak for themselves. Your lawyer will make proper use of them at the appropriate time. The simple fact is that, frequently, when you are overcome or seriously affected by emotional concerns, you are unable to present a full and clear explanation of the facts. Leave emotional appeals for your lawyer to make to the jury.

☞ Bring all documents or writings which are, or may be, important to your claim or defense, and tell your lawyer the point, or points, to which they are important.

☛ Identify all documents in the possession of third parties which are, or may be, important to your claim or defense, and tell your lawyer the point, or points, to which they are important.

☛ If you have a claim, specifically state the date on which you believe you were wronged by your opponent. That date may have legal importance.

☛ If you have a claim, specifically state how you have been damaged by the act, or the failure to act, of your opponent. If there are documents (e.g., bills, invoices, contracts, etc.), which refer to that damage, show them to your lawyer.

☛ If you are a defendant in a pending lawsuit, provide all information regarding any possible claims you may have against your opponent, or any co-defendants or a third-party.

☛ If there are any documents which are potentially important to the matter, and which could be considered as undermining your claim or defense, identify them, and (if possible) explain why they should not be construed against you.

☛ If your lawyer asks a question and you do not understand the question, ask that it be repeated or rephrased, so that you can fully respond to it.

☛ In presenting your claim or defense to your lawyer, do not be judgmental. For example, do not judge for yourself what facts may or may not be important. Provide your lawyer with all of the facts which bear on the subject, and let the lawyer decide which facts are important and which are not. Keep in mind that the overall objective of the initial meeting is to make certain your lawyer knows all of the facts which may be important to your claim or defense. You must rely on your lawyer to determine what use, if any, can be made of those facts. If your lawyer does not know all of the important facts within your knowledge, he or she will not be able to make that determination.

WHAT TO ASK YOUR LAWYER

After you have made the above presentation:

☛ Ask your lawyer whether there is additional information which is required to evaluate or present your claim or defense. If so, supply it, if you can, as soon as possible.

☛ Ask the lawyer for his or her evaluation of your chances for success. Of course, frequently, the lawyer may not be in a position to provide you with such an evaluation; or, if he or she can provide you with some estimate, it will not be one which is guaranteed. There can be many reasons for your lawyer's inability to provide this guidance; these are not important here. However, you *can* ask, and the lawyer may often be able to provide *some* information on the subject. For example, the lawyer may be able to advise you that you have very little chance of success. With that advice, you are in a better position to determine whether you wish to invest further time and money on the case.

☛ Ask your lawyer if there are any additional facts which would help your case. There may be things which you thought were unimportant which are actually crucial to your case. Once you know what is important you can search your records and your memory for facts which you previously ignored.

☛ Ask the lawyer to explain what *exposure* you have in pursuing your claim or defense. By exposure is meant what loss, if any, you might suffer in pursuing your claim or defense. The determination of that question depends on the types of claims or defenses which are present, the type of fee arrangement you have with your lawyer, the time involved and whether you are successful in pursuing your claim or defense. However, the **general** forms of exposure you may face include:

- **Your** attorney's fees. Initially, this form of exposure depends on the type of fee arrangement you have with your lawyer. Fee arrangements, and the subject of fees, generally, are discussed more fully later in this Chapter. Usually, fee arrangements are either *fixed* or *contingent*.

  In a fixed fee arrangement, you will pay your lawyer for services rendered either on an hourly basis (at a fixed rate per hour) or at a fixed, total sum for the entire representation. In a contingent fee arrangement, your lawyer is paid only if you are successful in pursing your claim or defense, usually from the amount recovered from your opponent. This type of fee arrangement is usually found only where you are plaintiff, and where success on your claim will result in your opponent having to pay an amount of damages (from which fees for your lawyer are taken).

The central difference between a fixed fee arrangement and a contingent one is that, in a fixed arrangement you are obligated to pay your lawyer's fees whether or not you are successful on your claim or defense, while in a contingent arrangement you are not obligated to pay your lawyer a fee unless you are successful (and the fee is actually paid by your opponent, from the monies collected on your claim).

In some cases, if your fee arrangement is a fixed one, and you are ultimately successful on your claim or defense, you may have a right to seek an award of attorneys' fees from your opponent, reimbursing you for the fees you have paid (or are obligated to pay) your lawyer. In other cases, you do not have such a right. If you are ultimately successful, and you do have such a right, keep in mind that: (1) the award authorized by the court may not include the entire amount of attorney's fees which you have paid (or are obligated to pay); and (2) such an award is worthless if your opponent does not have the financial ability to pay the award. If you are unsuccessful on your claim or defense, you will lose the amount of fees you have paid (or are obligated to pay) your lawyer. Of course, you will have no exposure for fees if your fee arrangement is a contingent one. Ask your lawyer whether you are, or may be, entitled to an award of fees from your opponent if you are successful on your claim or defense.

- Your *opponent's* attorneys' fees. In some cases, if you are not ultimately successful on your claim or defense, your opponent may have the right to seek an award against you for the amount of attorneys' fees they have paid (or are obligated to pay) for the services of their lawyer. In other instances, they do not have such a right. If your opponent is ultimately successful, and there is such a right, the same qualifications described above apply.

- Your court costs. By *court costs* is meant costs other than attorney's fees, which you may be obligated to pay in pursuing your claim or defense. These include; for example, filing fees, administrative fees, fees for court reporter's services, service of legal documents (including subpoenas), costs in obtaining written transcripts of depositions, investigator's fees, and expert witness fees. If you are not successful on your claim or defense, you will have lost these monies. Generally, if you are ultimately successful on your claim or defense, you will be entitled to an award of certain of these costs from your opponent. However, if you are ultimately successful and you are entitled to such an award, keep in mind that: (1) the amount of the award may not include all of the costs you have paid (or are obligated to pay); and (2) again, such an award is worthless if your opponent does not have the financial ability to pay the award.

- Your *opponent's* court costs. In most instances, if you are not ultimately successful on your claim or defense, your opponent may be entitled to an award against you for the costs they have paid (or are obligated to pay). Again, such an award is subject to the same qualifications described above. Ask your lawyer if you have, or may have, exposure to such an award.

- *Compensatory damages.* Compensatory damages are, generally, those financial losses which have actually been suffered as a result of the act, or the failure to act, of another party. If you are defending against a claim (i.e., a defendant), and you are not successful in defending against it, you will be subject to entry of an award against you for the compensatory damages suffered by your opponent.

- *Punitive damages.* Punitive damages are generally awarded, not to compensate for an actual loss, but rather either as a form of punishment against the other party or to serve as a deterrent to others from engaging in the type of conduct which is complained of in a claim. If a claim for punitive damages is made against you (in addition to a claim for compensatory damages) and you are not successful in defending against that claim, you may be subject to an award for such damages over and above the award for compensatory damages.

- *Incidental expenses.* Pursuing a claim or defense in court, in most instances, will require you, and perhaps others (e.g., employees, family members, etc.), to spend time in such activities as reviewing pleadings, taking of depositions, and attendance at trial. In some instances, this loss of time may well represent an additional financial loss for you, which is generally not included in any award for costs (or compensatory damages) if you are successful on your claim or defense.

In your initial meeting with your lawyer, thoroughly discuss your potential exposure in your particular case. And, if you decide to pursue your claim or defense, specifically request that your lawyer advise you if the extent of that exposure ever changes during the course of the trial process. The significance of your exposure is explained later in this chapter. Keep in mind that, at the initial meeting, your lawyer may not be in a position to advise you of the specific nature or dollar amount of your exposure, simply because they are not capable of being calculated or even estimated at that time. However, ask the lawyer to be as specific as possible. At the very least, your lawyer can advise you as to whether you may be liable for your opponent's legal fees if you are unsuccessful, and give you some estimate of the fees and costs involved. In some cases, your exposure in pursuing or defending against a claim may be crucial to your decision as to whether you wish to pursue it or defend against it.

☞ Ask your lawyer's advice as to the desirability of considering a compromise (or *settlement*) of your claim or defense. If you are willing to consider a compromise, discuss the terms or conditions you would require in order to do so.

☞ If you have a claim, or if you are a defendant but have a counterclaim against your opponent, ask your lawyer what elements (or types) of damages might be recoverable if you were successful on your claim. On receiving that advice, ask whether there is additional information which should be provided to your lawyer on that subject, and, if so, provide it as soon as possible.

☞ All claims, and defenses to those claims, have certain legally recognized *factual* elements or points which must be established in order to pursue them in court. Whether you are pursuing a claim or a defense, ask what specific *factual* elements or points you must establish in order to prevail, and *how* or by what means they can be established (that is, through what types of witnesses or documents). With this advice, you may be able to assist your lawyer in gathering the proof necessary to successfully present your case.

☞ Ask for advice as to whether you should discuss the facts of your claim or defense with any third parties (i.e., friends, acquaintances, spouses, etc.) while the matter is pending. Most lawyers will advise you not to do so without the lawyer being present.

☞ If you wish to have the lawyer represent both you and another person (either a co-plaintiff or a co-defendant), ask whether there is any potential conflict of interest in the lawyer representing both persons. If the lawyer advises that there is a possibility of a conflict of interest, thoroughly review that subject with the lawyer. Do not consent to a *waiver* of any potential conflict without thoroughly understanding the potential disadvantages in such representation.

☛ Whether you are a plaintiff or a defendant, discuss with your lawyer the advantages and disadvantages of requesting a jury trial. This decision is often made based upon whether the facts or the law are on your side, and whether your side would look more sympathetic to a jury. For example, if you are a plaintiff claiming damages for personal injuries, a jury would be more likely to sympathize with your pain and suffering than would a judge who hears such cases every day. On the other hand, if you represent a large business suing a small competitor over a complicated copyright issue, you may prefer a judge who understands copyright law and will follow it, over a jury which may get confused as to the applicable law and be sympathetic to a small company.

In making a decision in this matter, you should follow your lawyer's advice. He or she knows what kind of impression your case will make on a judge or jury.

Discuss these with your lawyer, and before you make a decision, make certain that you thoroughly understand the advantages and disadvantages. (In some instances, for legal reasons, you may have no choice as to whether your case will be decided by a judge or a jury. Your lawyer will advise you if such is the case).

☛ Ask whether it will be necessary (or desirable) to employ expert witnesses in order to present your claim or defense. If so, you may be in a position to assist your lawyer in locating such experts. Moreover, you will wish to discuss with the lawyer the potential costs involved in presenting such witnesses. The subject of experts can be important to your case and is dealt with in more detail later in this book.

A final point with regard to the initial meeting with your lawyer: If you intend to pursue a claim in which you wish to obtain an award of damages against your opponent, discuss with your lawyer the "collectibility" of such an award. Collectibility means whether, if you are successful on your claim, you will actually recover (receive) the amount of your damages from your opponent. An award of damages is worthless unless it is collectible from your opponent (i.e., your opponent has sufficient assets to pay the award). This is a problem area for several reasons.

First, neither you nor your lawyer are often in a position to actually know whether any award obtained will be collectible. For example, although your claim is against a large corporation or an individual who appear to be wealthy, you may discover that they are not after you have obtained your award. Of course, there are numerous reasons for this possibility, which need not be discussed here. However, do not merely assume that if you are successful in obtaining an award for damages, it will be collectible. Keep in mind that the mere fact that a corporation or an individual appears to be financially sound or prosperous does not mean that they are, in fact, financially sound or prosperous.

Frequently, there are several avenues available to your lawyer which may be used to gain at least some information regarding collectibility. If a question exists on the subject, review these possible avenues with your lawyer, and pursue them as soon as possible, preferably, before you commit to pursuing your claim. For example, you may have a valid claim for an award of $10,000, $25,000, $50,000, or several hundred thousand dollars. However, if that claim is not collectible, it would make no sense to pursue it, even though it is a valid one, since you would be "throwing good money after bad."

Keep in mind that there are many ways to conceal assets and there is a whole industry teaching people how to protect their assets. If you believe your opponent has considerable assets but it appears that they have few or none, you may want to do some research. They may have transferred their assets to their spouse or children or into an offshore trust. If you have any evidence that they may have more assets than they claim, by all means, point it out to your lawyer. You may also wish to hire a private investigator to research their assets.

ATTORNEY'S FEES AND COSTS

The subject of attorney's fees and costs is of the utmost importance to you, for two reasons:

1. The amount or extent of fees and costs you will be obligated to pay in pursuing your claim or defense may well decide or govern whether you wish to pursue it in the first place; and

2. If you do decide to pursue your claim or defense, you will wish to do what you can to keep fees and costs to a minimum, without jeopardizing your chances for success.

In order to address and evaluate these two concerns, you should be aware of the methods by which charges for fees and costs are usually determined. Generally, lawyers are compensated under five types of fee arrangements:

1. *Flat fee.* A flat, or fixed, fee of a certain amount.

2. *Contingent fee.* A contingent fee, based solely on a percentage of any recovery for damages made on your behalf (i.e., the lawyer looks to your opponent for his or her attorney's fees, and, if no such recovery is obtained, you will owe the lawyer nothing for fees).

3. *Hourly fee.* An hourly fee for the amount of time the lawyer spends working on your case;

4. *Combination.* In some instances, a combination of one or more of the foregoing arrangements. (For example, the lawyer may enter into a fee arrangement requiring payment of a flat or fixed fee of a certain amount together with a percentage of any recovery for damages made on your behalf, or, if you are a defendant, a percentage of the amount of monies which the lawyer saves you from having to pay on the opponent's claim.); and

5. *Reasonable fee.* In some cases, the lawyer's fee may be calculated on the basis of a *reasonable* fee. In this type of arrangement, the lawyer's fee is not finally calculated until the conclusion of the litigation. The lawyer calculates the fee owed based on a variety of factors, including the number of hours he or she devoted to the case, the complexity of the case, the benefit you derived from their services, etc. Infrequently, whether you are a plaintiff or a defendant, if you are successful on your claim or defense, a statute, rule or contract may provide for including in any verdict or

judgment on your behalf a reasonable attorneys' fee for your lawyer. If so, the lawyer may agree to compensation on that basis alone.

Ask on what basis the lawyer is to be compensated. If the basis is other than a fixed or a contingent fee, ask for an estimate of the fees you may be obligated to pay in pursuing your claim or defense. As with the concept of "chances for success," your lawyer may not be able to provide you with a reliable estimate as to fees. However, they might be in a position to do so. You have nothing to lose, and, perhaps, something to gain by asking.

In addition to fees, ask what other costs you will, or may, be obligated to pay in pursuing your claim or defense. As with fees, the lawyer may be unable to provide a reliable estimate, particularly at the initial meeting because of various elements of uncertainty. However, ask for an estimate. The lawyer may be in a position to provide a meaningful range of anticipated costs.

At the initial meeting, make certain that you are absolutely clear as to the type of fee arrangement which will be involved. On this point, a few additional suggestions:

☛ Enter into a *written* fee and cost agreement with your lawyer (detailing the fee, or the method by which the fee will be calculated, anticipated costs, etc.).

☛ The written agreement should specify exactly (as best as is reasonably possible) what services are to be performed by the lawyer on your behalf. (For example, does the fee arrangement include services performed in connection with an appeal, or is it limited to only services performed at the trial court level?)

☛ If your fee and cost agreement with the lawyer is not a flat or fixed fee, or a contingent fee, request that you be provided monthly, written statements for services rendered and costs incurred. This is a standard method of billing by lawyers, and it will assist you in monitoring the attorneys' fees and costs which you are obligated to pay during the progress of the case. If, at some point, you determine the fees and costs are approaching an amount in excess of what you wish to pay in pursuing your claim or defense, you may simply decide to abandon the matter, pay whatever fees and costs you currently owe, and cut your losses. Unless you receive monthly billings, you will not be in a position to consider this possibility.

☛ If you have questions after being advised of the fee and cost arrangement which is to be used, ask them. It is your money.

After the initial meeting with your lawyer, take a few moments to review the information you provided at the meeting and to digest any advice given by your lawyer. If you discover that you omitted important facts, or provided facts which are inaccurate, incomplete or misleading, immediately provide that information to your lawyer. If you have provided a written narrative to your lawyer, and it should be corrected in light of your review, correct it. If you are confused as to any matter discussed at the meeting, clear up that confusion with your lawyer as soon as possible.

Do You Wish to Pursue Your Case?

Once you have completed your discussion of each of the subjects previously identified in this chapter with your lawyer at the initial meeting, you must now decide whether you wish to pursue your claim or defense. At this point, you should review the discussion of this subject in the section on "What Is Winning?" in chapter 1.

Following Up On Your Case

Once you have retained a lawyer to represent you, you owe it to yourself to "stay on top of," or monitor, the progress of your case.

In monitoring the progress of your case, certain fundamental rules apply:

☛ Request that copies of all pleadings (that is, documents which are filed either on your own behalf or on behalf of your opponent in the case) be forwarded to you for review, analysis, and suggestions.

☛ Ask your lawyer to advise you as to the time and date at which important hearings will be held in your case, and, assuming your lawyer agrees, attend any such hearings. When attending any hearing, say nothing without the approval of your lawyer.

☛ Throughout the course of the trial process, periodically ask your lawyer in what manner, if any, you can help in the process. If you demonstrate to the lawyer that you are willing to help, the lawyer may recognize areas in which you could provide valuable assistance which he or she would not have recognized had you not offered your help. The result could be a possible reduction, perhaps a significant one, in your attorneys' fees and costs.

☞ Ask your lawyer to timely provide you with copies of all correspondence between your lawyer and the lawyer for your opponent. You may gain valuable information from such correspondence of which you were previously unaware, leading to your ability to make suggestions or provide information which would be of help to your lawyer. Most lawyers, particularly trial lawyers, make it a practice to provide you with such copies. However, if your lawyer does not, ask that he or she do so.

☞ Throughout the progress of the case, keep available some form of notebook to record any thoughts, points, or suggestions regarding the case as they occur to you. The notebook will be helpful in conveying any such information to your lawyer in a timely manner.

☞ Throughout the progress of the case, keep your lawyer informed of any travel plans; your availability; and where you can be reached if necessary. Your lawyer may need to contact you at any time on an important matter.

☞ Do not burden your lawyer with unimportant matters. Except in a contingency fee arrangement, doing so will merely increase the amount of attorney's fees you are ultimately obligated to pay your lawyer and, perhaps more importantly, you will unnecessarily distract your lawyer from presenting your claim or defense effectively.

☛ Remember that following up on your case does not necessarily mean that you must speak directly to your lawyer. Many of the suggestions offered here, and throughout this book, can be accomplished through speaking with the lawyer's secretary or paralegal personnel. Whenever possible, communicate through the lawyer's secretary (or paralegal), or by writing to the lawyer. In most cases, you will not be charged a fee or costs in speaking with a lawyer's secretary. If you speak with paralegal personnel you may be charged some fee, but at a charge less than would be charged for speaking with the lawyer. In addition, by communicating with the lawyer in writing, he or she will spend less time on the communication, thereby reducing fees.

PRE-TRIAL DISCOVERY AND OTHER PROCEEDINGS 5

TYPES OF DISCOVERY

After your claim or defense has been filed, your lawyer and the lawyer for your opponent will begin the *discovery* process (usually known as *pre-trial discovery*). This process (at least in theory) is quite simple and is designed to allow both you and your opponent to obtain as much information about your respective positions, in advance of trial, as possible.

In most cases, pre-trial discovery involves use of the following:

☞ ***Written interrogatories:*** These are written questions to the parties in the case concerning the issues which are required to be answered under oath. They may be used either by your lawyer or the lawyer for your opponent.

☞ ***Requests for admissions:*** Again, these can be used either by your lawyer or by the lawyer for your opponent, and request that you (or the other party) state whether or not you admit certain facts to be true.

☞ ***Requests for production of documents:*** Again, these can be used either by your lawyer or the lawyer for your opponent; they will generally request production by the opposing party of those documents which each party claims support or relate to their position.

☞ ***Depositions:*** Because of their importance, depositions will be addressed in more detail later. For now, depositions can be described merely as instances in which parties to the case, or witnesses, will be questioned under oath by the respective lawyers with a court reporter present who may later transcribe the proceeding.

OTHER PROCEEDINGS

Once you have filed your claim or defense in court, aside from the discovery process, there are a variety of events or proceedings which may well take place prior to the beginning of the actual trial on the claim or defense. You do not need to be thoroughly familiar with all of these matters, since, in large part, they will be handled by your lawyer. However, you should be aware of them, generally. These events or proceedings include:

☞ Analysis of the specific claim or defense actually filed, and any formal response filed by your opponent, for the purpose of determining whether additional, formal documents (i.e., *pleadings*) should be filed in order to protect your interests.

☞ Gathering of evidence to support your claim or defense, other than through discovery. For example, obtaining documents from third-parties, interviewing witnesses, employing experts, etc.

☞ Settlement negotiations. Such negotiations will be dealt with in detail later in this book. (Of course, in some instances, there may be no such negotiations, i.e., where either you or your opponent have no desire to settle or *compromise* the claim or defense. However, in most instances, prior to trial, some form of settlement negotiation is used, or at least should be used. If so, the negotiation will be handled by your lawyer, but, of course, only with your knowledge and input.)

HOW YOU CAN HELP DURING DISCOVERY

Before pre-trial discovery and other proceedings begin, make certain you understand your lawyer's *theory of the case*. All trial lawyers attempt to construct their theory of the case as soon as possible, and before completion of the initial pleadings (i.e., the complaint, answer, and defenses, etc.). Of course, because of the development of additional or new facts during the discovery stage, that theory may be amended or modified. However, prior to beginning discovery, your lawyer will have developed at least a preliminary theory of the case. Such a theory is simply an outline of exactly what your claim or defense is, how it can be proven in court, and what discovery may be necessary in order to assist in presenting your claim or defense. Unless you are aware of and fully understand that theory, you cannot effectively assist your lawyer in pursuing it.

After you are made aware of your lawyer's theory of the case, there are several ways in which you can help your lawyer. These are:

☛ First, ask your lawyer how you can be of help in preparing your case for trial. For example, the lawyer may request that you provide a written narrative, as previously discussed, if you have not already provided one, or that you assist in interviewing witnesses, or in obtaining important documents, etc. Frequently, your lawyer may not require your assistance in such matters. However, remember that any task you can perform which reduces the amount of time your lawyer is required to spend on preparing your case may reduce your attorney's fees.

☛ At the initial meeting with your lawyer (or soon thereafter), you will have already identified, at least preliminarily, all potential witnesses and significant documents. Throughout the pre-trial process, if appropriate, update that information as it becomes available.

☛ Thoroughly analyze all pleadings which have been filed, or will be filed, to make certain you understand them, and to determine whether they require additional investigation. If so, immediately advise your lawyer of that fact.

☛ If, at any time during the pre-trial process, you discover that you provided (or may have provided) inaccurate, misleading, or incomplete information to your lawyer, immediately bring that fact to their attention.

☛ As noted above, one of the avenues of discovery is written interrogatories. Written interrogatories are merely questions, in writing, to which the person receiving them must respond, also in writing, and under oath. Customarily, both plaintiffs and defendants send written interrogatories to each other. Since the answers to these interrogatories can be used at trial, make certain that, if you are responding to them, your answers are complete and accurate. If, after answering interrogatories, you discover you may have provided inaccurate, misleading or incomplete answers, immediately bring that fact to your lawyer's attention.

☞ In responding to a request for production of documents, make certain that you have provided your lawyer with all documents which have been requested of you by your opponent. If, after responding to such a request, you discover additional documents which should have been disclosed under the previous request, immediately bring that fact to the attention of your lawyer.

☞ Carefully review and analyze all pleadings filed by your opponent (particularly answers to interrogatories and responses to requests for admissions) to determine whether they contain inaccurate or misleading information or are incomplete. If they do contain such information or are incomplete, bring that fact to the attention of your lawyer immediately. In doing so, point out, specifically, *what* information is inaccurate or misleading or incomplete, *why* it is inaccurate, misleading or incomplete, and *how* it can be demonstrated, shown or proved to be defective in one or more of those categories. Follow the same procedure with respect to a deposition of your

65

opponent and a deposition of any key witness for your opponent.

In performing this task, do not be overly selective or judgmental: identify all points in these categories which you find. It may be that a particular point you raise may not be legally or factually important. However, that determination is for your lawyer to make, and if he or she is not aware of the point, they cannot make it. Of course, your lawyer will be performing the same task. However, two heads may well be better than one.

Finally, if you make such points regarding pleadings or depositions, bring them to the attention of your lawyer in writing, rather than orally. A written communication may well save time, thereby reducing legal fees, will lessen the chance of miscommunication, and will provide a ready reference for later use.

☞ Prior to trial, your lawyer will no doubt take the deposition of your opponent and of any key witnesses. Well in advance of the actual taking of the depositions, provide your lawyer with a written outline of the points you believe should be covered Some of these points may be legally unimportant, however, let your lawyer decide. If these depositions are transcribed, review them as soon as possible, and follow the suggestions above regarding the review and analysis of pleadings.

☞ You may be in a position to assist your lawyer in interviewing key witnesses whom you believe will support your case. If so, offer that assistance. For example, you may have a personal relationship with a potential witness who may be reluctant to speak with your lawyer. You may be in a better position than your lawyer to obtain from that witness the information desired by your lawyer. Or, perhaps a potential witness would be more comfortable with you present at an interview by your lawyer. In addition, your lawyer may intend to have certain witnesses interviewed, at least initially, by an investigator. By offering to conduct such interviews yourself, you may avoid that expense. Of course, for any number of reasons, your lawyer may prefer either to conduct such interviews themselves or through an investigator.

☞ You may be in a position to assist your lawyer in developing evidence in support of your case. For example, it may be necessary to contact various third-parties in an effort to locate important documents. Such searches can be time consuming. If you can conduct them, offer to do so.

☞ If your lawyer believes photos of a particular subject would be helpful in presenting your case, and you are in a position to take them, offer to do so. (Your lawyer may prefer they be taken by a professional, or by a third-party).

☞ You may be able to help your lawyer in drafting appropriate requests to produce to be addressed to your opponent, by suggesting documents to be included, and assuring that they are accurately described. Similarly, if important documents are in the possession of a third-party, your lawyer may be required to obtain them through a *subpoena*. You may be able to assist in drafting the subpoena. If your lawyer does direct a request to produce to your opponent, or a subpoena to a third-party, you will be able to assist by reviewing any documents produced in response to them to determine whether all documents called for were, in fact, produced.

Here are two final suggestions:

1. From time to time during the pre-trial process, your opponent's lawyer may request that your lawyer agree to a continuance of a particular hearing or an extension of time within which to perform a certain act. You may have an objection to the request, usually because it will involve a delay in ultimate resolution of the case. While each such request is different, depending on the circumstances, rely on the advice of your lawyer in determining whether or not to agree to the request.

2. During the pre-trial process, your opponent, through their counsel, may request that you and your counsel enter into a *stipulation* as to some matter. A stipulation is a formal agreement regarding a matter important to the case. Usually, it concerns an agreement between you and your opponent, and your respective lawyers, that a certain fact need not be proved at trial. Stipulations can be quite complex and are important. Do not agree to a stipulation proposed by your opponent without a thorough analysis and discussion with your lawyer.

DEPOSITIONS

Importance of Depositions

As previously discussed, in most instances, plaintiffs and defendants depose (through their respective lawyers) each other, as well as potential key witnesses for each side. If the opposing lawyer wishes to take your deposition, the event is a very important one, for which you should be thoroughly prepared. The taking of your deposition by your opponent's lawyer is important for several reasons.

Your effectiveness at the deposition (i.e., your demeanor, appearance, directness, truthfulness, believability, etc.) will be judged by your opponent's lawyer. That judgment is important since it may well determine whether you are able to obtain an acceptable settlement of your claim or defense (assuming, of course, you wish to settle or compromise your claim or defense). Why? Because, in making the determination of whether to propose a possible settlement or compromise, your opponent's lawyer will place great emphasis on his or her judgment as to your effectiveness at the deposition since that fact has a bearing on how effective you will be as a witness at trial.

The responses you make to questions asked during the deposition can be used as evidence at trial. If a particular answer you give to a question at the deposition differs from an answer you give to the same, or a similar, question at trial, your opponent's lawyer may well be able to use that fact to your disadvantage.

Assuming your *credibility* (i.e., believability) is important at trial, any matter which concerns your credibility is significant. One of the methods most frequently used by lawyers at trial to show a lack of credibility in a witness is to point out that the testimony of the witness (be it you or some other key witness) at trial differs from that given at deposition. Keep in mind that the significance of the difference is in the eye of the beholder (i.e., the judge or jury). What may seem to be a minor difference to you, may be perceived by the fact-finder as a major difference. The more significant the difference, the greater the potential damage to credibility.

The differences between deposition testimony and trial testimony which may have an impact on credibility generally take two forms:

1. A statement made at deposition which is (or apparently is) contradictory to a statement on the same subject at trial

2. Important testimony which is given at trial but was not disclosed at pre-trial deposition, and which, at least arguably, should have been disclosed at deposition in response to a particular question.

A few examples will illustrate these points. First, assume that at deposition, you state that a particular event occurred at a particular time. At trial, however, you testify that the event occurred at a different time. Or, assume that, during deposition, you testify that particular persons were present at an event, while, at trial, you testify that those persons were not present. An example of the second form of difference is that at deposition, you are asked why you committed a certain act, and you respond by giving certain reasons. At trial, however, when asked the same question, you respond by giving different, or additional, reasons why you committed the act.

In legal terms, such inconsistencies are called *prior inconsistent statements*. You should also note that prior inconsistent statements are not limited to statements given during a deposition, but can be based on any statements made at any time. (This is the basis for a prior suggestion in this book that you not discuss the facts of the case with third parties without the knowledge of your lawyer.) The theory behind the prior inconsistent statement concept is that, by making a prior statement (at deposition) which is inconsistent (or arguably inconsistent) with a statement made at trial, it can be concluded that the witness is not credible (i.e., believable). Either form of a prior inconsistent statement can seriously damage (if not totally destroy) your chances for success on your claim or defense.

The potential difficulties of the prior inconsistent statement concept (at least insofar as it applies to your deposition testimony) can be substantially, if not totally, eliminated by adequate preparation for your deposition. I say this because rarely, if ever, can a person describe an event on one occasion (at deposition), and later, on another occasion (trial), describe that same event without there being some inconsistency. The point is that it is to your advantage to make certain any such inconsistencies are both minimal and minor. A few suggestions, then, as to: (a) how to prepare for the taking of your deposition, and (b) how to respond to questions at your deposition.

Preparing for Your Deposition

In preparing for your deposition:

☞ Carefully review all of the pleadings which have been filed in the action. In analyzing these documents, make certain you have all of them. Frequently, *amendments*, i.e., additions or changes, to such pleadings are filed throughout the course of litigation. Those amendments are just as important as the initial pleadings.

☞ Ask your lawyer what specific subjects he or she expects will be addressed at the deposition.

☞ Carefully review your narrative of the facts.

☞ If you expect that the deposition will include questions regarding documents, carefully review them.

☞ If possible, make certain you have set aside ample time to allow you to be thoroughly rested before the deposition begins.

☞ If you are asserting a claim for damages, ask your lawyer's advice as to the appropriate method of responding to questions, if they are asked, regarding this subject. Often, the subject of damages can be quite complex legally, and, in some cases, questions on the subject should be responded to not by you, but your lawyer. Follow the lawyer's advice.

☞ On occasion, at deposition the opposing lawyer may ask you a *hypothetical* question. Hypothetical questions are those which require you to assume certain facts or concepts. These facts or concepts may, or may not, be true, accurate, complete, etc. Ask your lawyer whether you should expect to be asked such questions, and, if so, ask for advice as to how you should respond appropriately. (It may well be that, if such questions are asked of you, your lawyer will intervene, and refuse to permit you to answer. Rely on your lawyer's advice.)

☛ If pre-trial discovery depositions of your opponent (or key witnesses) have been taken, or your lawyer has obtained written statements from important witnesses, prior to the taking of your deposition, carefully review (or re-review) those materials prior to your deposition.

☛ Confirm your understanding of the theory of the case with your lawyer to make certain you do not unknowingly contradict that theory at your deposition. In addition, confirm your understanding of your opponent's theory of the case with your lawyer. Usually, prior to the taking of your deposition, your lawyer will be in a position to advise you of that theory. Of course, that advice may be preliminary, since, as with your theory, your opponent's may be amended or modified as a result of the discovery process. The point is that, prior to your deposition, as best you can, you must be thoroughly familiar not only with your theory of the case, but also that of your opponent. Otherwise, at your deposition you cannot effectively support your theory or, if appropriate, rebut that of your opponent.

☛ Ask your lawyer what form of dress is appropriate for your attendance at the deposition. Your appearance may well have an impact on the opposing lawyer's view of your potential effectiveness as a witness at trial.

Answering Questions at Your Deposition

At your deposition, consider the following points:

☞ Your answers to questions should be clear, complete, and concise.

☞ Listen carefully to a question before responding.

☞ Do not answer a question which you do not understand. If you do not understand the question, before responding, ask the opposing lawyer to repeat or re-phrase the question. For several reasons, lawyers frequently ask questions at depositions which are not understandable. Do not be reluctant to ask that the question be re-phrased.

☞ Do not attempt to answer a question when you do not actually know the answer. Simply state that you do not know the answer.

☞ Unless you are asking the opposing lawyer to re-phrase a question, do not answer a question with a question.

☞ Unless you have been advised by your lawyer to do so, do not volunteer information which is not called for by the question.

☞ In responding to a question, do not engage in guesswork, speculation or conjecture. Either you know the answer or you do not.

☞ Do not assume that you should know an answer merely because the opposing lawyer asks a question of you. Frequently, lawyers ask questions at depositions when they have no reason whatsoever to believe that the deponent (you) knows the answers.

- ☛ If you believe you do know the answer to a question asked, but your knowledge is based on information obtained from a third-party or a document; make clear in responding that they are the source of your knowledge.

- ☛ Think before you respond to a question.

- ☛ In responding to questions, do not become impatient. That trait may be viewed by opposing counsel as adversely effecting your credibility.

- ☛ Do not be evasive in your responses to questions; you either know the answer or you do not.

- ☛ Do not argue with opposing counsel, on any matter or subject.

- ☛ Do not allow yourself to become angry or emotional. Again, opposing counsel may well view this trait as damaging to your credibility, and, in any event, it will serve no useful purpose.

- ☛ If you are asked a question, and you wish to discuss it with your lawyer before answering, say so. Your lawyer will ask for a brief recess for that purpose. (Of course, you should not make this a practice, and should only request such a conference when absolutely necessary. Otherwise, you will give the impression of being "coached" on your answers by your lawyer, which adversely impacts on your credibility.)

- ☛ Do not be sarcastic in your responses. Again, that trait may damage your credibility.

- ☛ Never respond to a question concerning the contents of a document, of any kind, without having that document before you, reviewing it, and understanding the specific question being asked. If asked a question concerning a document, you have a right to review that document at that time, before responding. This suggestion applies no matter how familiar you are with the document because your interpretation of its contents may be very different from that of opposing counsel.

☛ Do not volunteer to seek out further information or produce documents which are not presently in your possession. If such a procedure is appropriate, your lawyer will respond accordingly.

☛ Do not be rushed in responding to a question. Usually, of course, your lawyer will protect you on this point. However, if he or she does not, protect yourself.

☛ If you are asked a question which would require you to give further thought or analysis, or review certain documents, do not be reluctant to say so. For instance, "I would have to think about that matter further before responding," or words to that effect.

☛ In responding to a question, do not exaggerate. Exaggeration will almost always come back to haunt you.

☛ In responding to a question, do not provide information which is obviously not important or not responsive to the question.

☛ Obviously, do not use foul or profane language in responding to questions.

☛ If, at any time during the deposition, you become upset, extensively tired, or are in need of a break for any reason, do not be reluctant to request one. If, although unlikely, the opposing lawyer objects, insist on taking the break unless your lawyer specifically advises against it.

☛ In responding to questions, avoid characterizations, i.e., "X is a liar," "X is a thief," etc. The facts, not words, show such characteristics.

☛ Do not allow the opposing lawyer to bully or harass you. Such instances rarely arise. If they do, no doubt your lawyer will protect you from them. However, if your lawyer does not, protect yourself.

☛ If you are asked a question which you believe is repetitious (i.e., you have already been asked the question, and responded), be patient, at least at first, and respond again. Of course, if the opposing lawyer consistently engages in repetitive questions, your lawyer will object and may even direct you not to answer. Rely on your lawyer's advice. Frequently, questions which may appear repetitive to you, legally, may not be repetitive. Moreover, pay special attention to questions which appear to be repetitive because they may well indicate a key point, or points, in the view of the opposing lawyer. That knowledge may be helpful to you and your lawyer.

☛ If you are asserting a claim for damages, pay particular attention to questions concerning those damages, and, to the best of your ability, respond fully.

☛ Be particularly careful in responding to hypothetical questions, discussed earlier in this chapter. Although the general subject of hypothetical questions has been previously addressed, the subject warrants further explanation here. Earlier, it was suggested that, prior to the taking of your deposition, you seek your lawyer's advice as to whether such questions might be asked at your deposition, and, if so, what responses were appropriate. If your lawyer anticipated that such questions might be asked at your deposition, no doubt he or she would have advised you (a) not to answer such a question without allowing them an opportunity to object to the question; (b) if no objection is made, to listen carefully to the question; and (c) if you cannot answer the question as asked, you should make that point clear at the deposition. A hypothetical question is based on **assumed** facts. However, the danger of hypothetical questions is that they may be based on a supposed fact, or facts, which are not true. If this is the case, your lawyer should be in a position to object to the question asked of you on that ground, and you will not be required to answer the question. A hypothetical question may also suffer from another defect—to answer it, one might be required to consider **additional** facts which have not been included in the question. Again, if such is the case, your lawyer may enter an appropriate objection, and direct you not to answer the question. However, here you may be able to assist your lawyer by either consulting with your lawyer privately, and suggesting those facts which must be included in the hypothetical in order for you to answer it, or by making that point to opposing counsel. The safest course is to consult with your lawyer, rather than to suggest to opposing counsel what additional facts must be included in the hypothetical before you are in a position to answer it.

☞ On occasion, the opposing lawyer may ask you a question regarding a prior conversation with your lawyer. Before responding, make certain your lawyer agrees that the subject is proper for disclosure. As you probably know, absent a waiver, conversations between a lawyer and a client which are important to the representation in question are generally privileged from disclosure. However, there are certain exceptions to this rule. For example, in some instances it is proper to ask questions of you concerning information you provided your lawyer which subsequently appears in pleadings filed in the case, or disclosed to third parties. Rely on your lawyer's advice as to whether to respond to such questions.

☞ Before responding to a question, allow your lawyer adequate time to make an objection to the question asked (i.e., do not answer the question so quickly that your lawyer does not have adequate time to make an objection). Moreover, your lawyer may wish not only to object, but to direct you not to answer the question.

☞ If your lawyer does make an objection to a question asked but does not direct you not to answer, listen carefully to the objection and do not respond unless you understand the objection. That objection may assist you in answering the question appropriately. A further word about objections, generally. There are two types of objections which a lawyer may make to a question during a deposition: (a) an objection which, nevertheless, permits you to answer the question after the objection has been made a matter of record; and (b) an objection resulting in an instruction by your lawyer that you not answer the question. Obviously, if your lawyer instructs you not to answer the question, follow that advice. In short, at a deposition there are legal considerations which, under certain circumstances, permit you to be required to answer a particular question, even if your lawyer makes an objection to it. There are other questions, however, which, on proper objection, you are not required to answer. Rely on the advice of your lawyer.

☞ Be especially careful to correct the opposing lawyer if he or she asks a question based on a misstatement of your answer to a previous question. Usually, such an occurrence is entirely unintentional. Occasionally, however, it is not. In either event, do not answer a question based on a misstatement of your prior testimony, at least without pointing out the misstatement within the question.

☞ After having answered a question, if you realize later in the deposition that your previous answer was inaccurate, incomplete or misleading, attempt to correct or amend that answer as appropriate.

Frequently, your deposition will be transcribed (i.e., typed by the court reporter) and furnished to your lawyer. If so, review the transcript and determine whether your answers were complete and accurate. If they were not, immediately advise your lawyer of that fact. And, if you note what you believe to be errors in the transcript, immediately bring those errors to the attention of your lawyer.

PRE-TRIAL STATEMENTS

Frequently, once pre-trial proceedings are completed, the judge presiding over the case may require that a *pre-trial statement* (or similar document) be filed by your lawyer. A pre-trial statement is usually a written statement in which your lawyer briefly summarizes your version of your claim or defense, any stipulations which have been entered into, the issues to be resolved by the fact-finder, and an identification of all witnesses whom you anticipate calling at trial, as well as all documents which you intend to offer into evidence at trial.

These last two points are quite important. Make certain you review any such pretrial statement to be offered by your lawyer before it is offered, to assure that it includes all witnesses whom you expect to call at trial, together with all documents you expect to offer into evidence. Frequently, such pleadings are prepared at the last minute, in a rush, and there is a possibility that any witnesses who are omitted from the statement will not be permitted to testify at trial, and any document which is omitted will not be allowed to be introduced at trial in support of your case.

SETTLEMENT NEGOTIATIONS

Assuming you are willing to settle, or compromise, your claim or defense under certain terms or conditions, settlement negotiations will be important. In approaching settlement negotiations, and throughout that process, a few suggestions:

☛ Leave your emotions at home. In any litigation, settlement considerations should be viewed as a business judgment.

☞ Thoroughly analyze each of those factors previously discussed regarding whether you wish to pursue your case.

☞ Make certain your lawyer is aware of all of the terms and conditions under which you are agreeable to a settlement.

☞ Make certain you clearly ask your lawyer to advise you of all of the possible disadvantages of settlement.

☞ Do not enter into any stipulation or agreement for settlement unless it includes all of the terms and conditions which you understand are applicable.

☞ Do not enter into any stipulation or agreement for settlement unless you fully understand each and every one of its terms and conditions.

☞ During settlement negotiations, keep in mind that such negotiations are subject to the law applicable to contracts. Specifically, keep in mind that, if your opponent makes an unqualified offer of settlement, and you either directly reject it or respond to it by making a counter-settlement offer, your opponent's initial offer no longer exists. For example, if you later change your mind, and wish to accept the initial offer of your opponent, you can no longer do so (unless, of course, your opponent is willing to renew the offer). Often, offers of settlement are qualified by a deadline; if they are not accepted within a certain period of time, they automatically expire or are considered as withdrawn. On occasion, an offer of settlement may expire or be considered as withdrawn after the lapse of a *reasonable time*. If an offer of settlement is made by your opponent, ask your lawyer when it expires, and act accordingly.

☞ If you are a plaintiff, keep in mind that the mere fact that you are willing to discuss the possibility of settlement does not indicate that you are admitting or conceding that your claim lacks merit. Valid claims are settled every day for less than the amount the plaintiff may be entitled to, for practical reasons (usually to avoid further costs and delay). Similarly, if you are a defendant, the mere fact that you are willing to discuss a possible settlement does not mean that you are admitting or conceding that the plaintiff's claim has any merit or that you did, or did not do, something wrong. Invalid claims are settled every day by defendants in order to avoid further costs, expenses and delay. If a settlement is reached, that fact is not an admission of any kind against either party. And, in most cases, if a party wishes, the terms of a settlement can be kept in confidence, i.e. remain secret between the parties.

☞ Your lawyer will advise you of any formal offers of settlement received from opposing counsel. Often, however, lawyers for the parties in litigation may have informal, preliminary conversations regarding possible settlement. Ask your lawyer to advise you of any such conversations. They may provide useful information in evaluating your case or be of use later if formal settlement discussions take place.

Very few cases ever get to trial. Many are settled some time earlier, often minutes before the trial is to begin. There is a reason for this. No matter how right your side is, no matter how strong your case, no matter how many witnesses you have, there is still a chance you will lose. Many factors enter into the final decision in a court case. The believability of the witnesses, the "fairness" of the claims, the mood of the judge or jury, the attitudes of the attorneys, the appearance of the parties, all enter into the decision process either consciously or unconsciously.

As stated elsewhere in this book, you may be well advised to seriously consider whether your interests would be best served by a settlement. You should discuss the possibility of settlement, and its advantages and disadvantages, with your lawyer.

If you do reach a settlement, usually you will be required to sign some form of a *release*. A release is an agreement (in fact, a contract) whereby one person gives up, or *waives*, any claims they have, or may have, against another, except as qualified in the release. Releases can be quite complex. In short, they are designed to put an end to a dispute or controversy. In litigation, they are designed to prevent the parties from raising new claims after a case has been settled.

Releases can be very important. Before you sign one, review it carefully with your lawyer, and sign it only with the approval of your lawyer. In reviewing a proposed release with your lawyer, make certain you understand exactly **what** claims are being released, and **who**, specifically, is being released. If the other party has, or may have, a claim against you, you will want to obtain an appropriate release from that party, which will be prepared or reviewed by your lawyer. With your lawyer's advice, you will make certain that the release includes all claims which have been, or could be, made against you.

SUMMARY JUDGMENTS

After the completion of the pre-trial discovery process, either your lawyer or your opponent's lawyer may file certain papers in an attempt to avoid the necessity of a full trial before the judge or jury. In most states, and in the federal courts, this attempt may be made by a *motion for summary judgment*.

While the subject of summary judgments can be quite complex legally, in substance, a motion for summary judgment argues that all necessary pre-trial discovery has been completed, all of the facts which are important to resolving the case are known, there is no dispute between the parties as to these facts, and that, when the law governing the case is applied to those facts, it is clear that one party or the other is entitled to a judgment in their favor.

If such a motion is granted, the case is concluded without a trial (subject to a possible appeal). In short, the case is over in the trial court, and there will be no trial conducted.

A trial is designed to provide a method by which to resolve **disputed** questions of **fact**. Since trials are designed to resolve **factual** disputes, one can see that, if the important facts are not in dispute, the only question which remains to be resolved is a **legal** one: when the applicable law is applied, which party is entitled to a verdict or judgment in their favor? (Of course, in many instances, there can be a legitimate dispute as to exactly what principles of law apply, however, that is a legal matter left to the respective lawyers and the judge.) So, one can see that, if there are no disputed questions of fact, there is no need for an actual trial in order to resolve the controversy.

A motion for summary judgment is designed to address this situation. If there are no disputed questions of fact, neither the parties, nor the public, should be put to the financial expense of conducting a trial. Generally, summary judgments are infrequently granted for two reasons. First, they are viewed with disfavor by the courts because they deprive one of the parties (i.e., the person against whom judgment is entered) of their "day in court." Second, usually, there are disputed questions of important fact.

With this background, one can see the importance of the concept of summary judgment to you, the client. That significance is two-fold. First, if you may be entitled to summary judgment, it is obviously to your advantage to pursue it, since you will avoid the expense of a trial. In the alternative, if your opponent files such a motion, and it is granted, you will be denied your day in court. You can help your lawyer with the subject of summary judgment in several ways.

First, at the conclusion of all necessary pre-trial discovery, you should consult with your lawyer as to whether such a motion should be filed on your behalf. Ultimately, you must rely on your lawyer to make that decision, since it is primarily a legal one.

No doubt your lawyer, on his or her own, will review that question. However, successful lawyers are busy and may unintentionally overlook this possibility. Frequently, analysis of this issue is quite complex, and requires thorough study. No competent lawyer will file such a motion haphazardly and without thorough consideration. So, if your lawyer does not initiate discussion of the subject, you should initiate it, to make absolutely certain that no possibility of obtaining an advantageous result in your behalf, at the lowest cost, is overlooked.

Second, if your opponent files such a motion, you may well be in a position to assist your lawyer in defeating it. Usually, such motions are based on the depositions and documents which have been obtained during the discovery process, as well as affidavits of various potential witnesses which are filed in support of the motion.

The party filing the motion (the *movant*) will attempt to show that these depositions, documents, and affidavits address all of the facts which are important to the case; and that those facts are undisputed. It is the responsibility of your lawyer, in attempting to defeat such a motion, to thoroughly analyze these matters, and to prepare to meet them at the hearing on the motion.

However, no competent trial lawyer is so egotistical that he or she would not welcome your assistance in preparing to attempt to defeat the motion. The most significant way in which you can assist your lawyer on this subject is to thoroughly review all of the depositions, documents, pleadings, and affidavits with a view toward determining two questions: (1) do the facts relied on by your opponent (which they contend are undisputed) include **all** of the facts important to the controversy; and (2) are the particular facts identified by your opponent as being **undisputed** actually undisputed.

In preparing to oppose the motion, your lawyer will address both questions. Usually, your opponent will set out in their motion the facts they contend are important and attempt to show why they are supposedly undisputed. If their motion does not do so, your lawyer will be in a position to advise you as to what contentions you can anticipate your opponent will argue. Of course, frequently, the issue of what facts are important in a particular case is a legal one which will be addressed by your lawyer. However, you can help defeat such a motion by:

1. offering your suggestions as to facts which you believe to be important and which are omitted from your opponent's discussion or argument; and,

2. pointing out any facts which your opponent claims are undisputed which are, in fact, disputed. In doing so, point out the source of your belief that a particular fact is in dispute. For example, a "fact" which your opponent claims to be undisputed may be shown to be disputed by reference to an answer given during a deposition, information found in answers to interrogatories or responses to requests to admit, or in documents produced by the parties.

You may also be able to assist your lawyer in determining whether there may be other, additional information which has not yet been made a matter of record, but which nevertheless creates a dispute as to particular facts. For example, in their motion, your opponent may state that a particular fact is undisputed, and, after reviewing all of the pertinent materials filed to date, you conclude that they are correct.

However, you are aware of a witness who can dispute that particular fact, but that witness has not yet been deposed nor given an affidavit on the point. Or, you are aware of a document which disputes the particular fact, but which has not yet been brought to the attention of your lawyer. In either event, you can assist your lawyer by pointing out this additional information, and, perhaps, assist in obtaining an appropriate affidavit from that witness or the document in question, which can then be filed with the court prior to a hearing on the motion.

Alternatively, if you are the movant, your opponent may file an affidavit in opposition to your motion which attempts to create a dispute as to a particular fact. If you are of the opinion that the affidavit does not create a dispute on that particular fact, immediately advise your lawyer of that fact, together with the reason, or reasons, for your position.

A word of caution: once a motion for summary judgment is filed by your opponent, usually there will be a rigid time frame imposed within which your lawyer must respond to it, by filing additional affidavits or documents, etc. Consequently, if you intend to assist your lawyer in attempting to defeat such a motion, you should do so as soon as possible and within whatever time limit is imposed.

TRIAL 6

THE TRIAL PROCESS

A trial is merely a method by which both sides, you and your opponent, are given an opportunity to present your respective positions to a supposedly unbiased third-party, either a judge or a jury, for resolution. In a civil case to be decided by a jury, the trial usually takes place in seven stages:

1. Jury selection
2. Opening arguments
3. Presentation of evidence by the parties
4. A *charge* conference, in which the trial judge and the lawyers for the respective parties determine what formal instructions will be given by the judge to the jury for guidance in arriving at its verdict
5. Closing arguments
6. Final instructions by the judge to the jury
7. The return of a verdict by the jury

In a civil case to be tried by the court (i.e., a non-jury trial), the process is identical, except that there is no selection of a jury or the necessity of jury instructions.

Depending on the circumstances, there may be additional proceedings which are conducted during the trial. For example, in a civil case, the plaintiff (the one asserting the claim in question) bears *the burden of proof*. If, for some legal reason, either the trial judge or the defendant's lawyer believe that the plaintiff has failed to meet the applicable burden of proof, a hearing (outside the presence of the jury) will be conducted on that subject. If, after that hearing is concluded, the judge is of the opinion that the plaintiff has not met its burden of proof, the judge will enter a judgment in favor of the defendant, and the trial is concluded at that point. If the judge believes the plaintiff has met the applicable burden of proof, the trial will proceed with the presentation of the defendant's evidence.

At the conclusion of the presentation of that evidence, the judge, either on his or her own or on motion of the defendant, can revisit the burden of proof issue. If the judge concludes that, considering all of the evidence presented, the plaintiff has failed to meet the applicable burden of proof, he or she will enter a judgment in favor of the defendant. If the judge believes the plaintiff has met the applicable burden of proof, and that there are factual disputes between the parties, the case will proceed with consideration by the jury, and, ultimately, the return of a verdict.

How You Can Help at Trial

With the above general outline of the trial process in mind, there are a number of ways in which you can help your lawyer win your case at this stage of the proceedings. Following are a few suggestions.

Jury Selection

Ask your lawyer if you can be of assistance in the jury selection process. Usually that process includes allowing the lawyers for the respective parties to ask questions of prospective jurors concerning their backgrounds and views on particular subjects. These questions are designed, at least in theory, to allow the selection of jurors who will be fair and impartial in deciding the case. You may have suggestions as to particular questions which might be asked of prospective jurors to determine the likelihood that they will, or will not, be fair and impartial. Of course, your lawyer must be the final decision-maker on what questions are asked. However, if you have suggestions, make them.

In some cases, all questioning of prospective jurors is done by the trial judge. In those cases, however, prior to trial the judge will usually permit the respective lawyers to submit, in writing, suggested questions to be asked of prospective jurors for consideration by the judge. If this procedure is to be followed, and you have suggestions as to questions which might be asked, provide them to your lawyer so that, if appropriate, they can be included in this written submission.

During the selection process, you may have some particular insight as to whether a particular prospective juror would, or would not, be fair and impartial. If you do, share that insight with your lawyer. In addition, you may have specialized knowledge concerning the occupational background of a particular prospective juror with which your lawyer is not familiar. That knowledge may be of assistance in determining possible personality traits which may be important in the selection process.

Obviously, jury selection is not a science, and, while your lawyer may well have experience which is helpful in selecting a fair and impartial jury, he or she will welcome any thoughts you may have on the subject. However, because of your lawyer's training and experience, you should follow his or her advice on the ultimate decision as to whether to accept or reject a particular juror, unless you have a very strong opinion to the contrary.

Documents to be Used as Evidence

If there are numerous documents which are important to the case, you may be in a position to assist your lawyer in organizing them for use at trial, and, at the trial, assisting the lawyer in locating specific documents at appropriate times. Again, ask your lawyer if you can assist in this regard.

Questions for Witnesses

Prior to trial discuss with your lawyer, at least generally, what factual points he or she intends to make at trial through the questioning of witnesses (including you). Most trial lawyers prepare an outline of their intended direct and cross-examination of anticipated witnesses in advance of trial (which is, of course, frequently amended or modified as the testimony unfolds from the witness stand). If your lawyer has prepared such an outline, ask to review it.

If you have suggestions, either as to questions you think are unwise or additional questions which might be asked, make them. Of course, your lawyer must make the final decision on what questions are to be asked of witnesses. However, your suggestions will be welcome, and may assist the lawyer in making certain no important points are overlooked. If you have more than a few suggestions, put them in writing. If your lawyer has not prepared an outline, ask for an oral summary. Again, if you have suggestions, make them. If you wish to offer assistance on the subject of questioning witnesses, keep in mind two points:

1. At the conclusion of the presentation of evidence stage of the trial, your lawyer will make a final argument to the fact-finder, in part, summarizing the important facts supporting your case. That argument must be based on facts or inferences from facts, established by the evidence at trial, either through the testimony of witnesses or the contents of documents. Facts or inferences from facts which have not been established at trial, even if true, cannot be argued by your lawyer in final argument.

2. Aside from legal issues, your case will be decided by a third-party, the fact-finder, based on the facts, or lack of facts, that they, not you or your lawyer, believe are important. Put another way, the fact-finder is not

necessarily bound by what you or your lawyer believe to be the important facts. Any trial lawyer can recall cases in which the fact-finder (particularly a jury) has rendered a verdict based on the absence of facts, that is, questions the fact-finder believed to be important, but were not answered by the evidence. Consequently, you may be able to assist your lawyer in attempting to avoid such a verdict by suggesting to your lawyer those questions which, if you were the fact-finder, you would wish to have answered by the evidence. Of course, in preparing for trial, and in presenting your case at trial, your lawyer will devote a great deal of attention to this subject. However, lawyers are human, and, again, it may be that "two heads are better than one."

There is a rule which applies to testimony which is so old that it is usually called *The Rule*. It is the *rule of sequestration*. This means that each witness can be asked to testify without the other witnesses being present. The purpose for the rule is to insure that witnesses testify as to what they remember, and do not base their testimony on what they have heard other witnesses say. Judges long ago learned that taking separate testimony from each witness is the best way to get to the truth.

Therefore, you may expect that during depositions or trial testimony, your lawyer or the other lawyer will ask the judge to "invoke the rule" and ask anyone who is not testifying to leave the room. This does not include parties to the case, since they are allowed to attend the entire proceeding.

Assisting at Trial

During the presentation of evidence stage, again, you may be able to assist your lawyer by suggesting questions which might be asked of witnesses, particularly where new, unanticipated issues have been raised during testimony. In making such suggestions, as much as possible, attempt to do so by writing a note to your lawyer, rather than orally. Your lawyer has a great responsibility in presenting your case, and trials are usually fast-paced. If you interrupt your lawyer's concentration while a witness is testifying in order to make a suggestion orally, the lawyer may become distracted, perhaps to your detriment. The lawyer cannot listen to both the testimony of the witness and you at the same time.

Most trial lawyers will follow a practice whereby, when the lawyer has concluded his or her intended examination of a witness, he or she will consult with you regarding any suggestions for further questions you may have before formally concluding the examination. Prior to trial, determine if your lawyer intends to follow this practice. If not, request that he or she do so.

Occasionally, new information (i.e., information not previously known to you or your lawyer) which could be damaging to your case may be disclosed for the first time at trial. If so, you may be in a position to assist your lawyer in locating witnesses or documentary evidence which will eliminate, or at least diminish, its damaging effect.

During the trial, take notes of important testimony. Those notes may be of assistance to your lawyer.

Spotting Prior Inconsistent Statements

Prior to trial, analyze all prior statements or deposition testimony which you have given, and determine if they contain inconsistencies, either with each other or with testimony you intend to give at trial. If such inconsistencies exist, be prepared to explain them at trial when you testify.

Also prior to trial, carefully review all depositions or other statements of potential witnesses. At trial, if a witness gives testimony which conflicts with that given on a prior occasion, and for some reason your lawyer overlooks that fact, you will be in a position to point out to your lawyer any such differences or inconsistencies. Of course, your lawyer bears the primary responsibility for accomplishing this task. However, you may be in a position to assist.

Your Testimony

If you are testifying and the trial judge asks a question of you, you must respond to it directly, concisely, and clearly (assuming it is not objected to by your lawyer). Never argue with the judge. If necessary, that is your lawyer's function, not yours. And, in answering the question, apply the same suggestions as to answering questions asked by opposing counsel at deposition which were discussed in chapter 5.

If, prior to trial, the opposing lawyer took your deposition, be prepared for the lawyer to question you at trial on subjects which he or she did not address at your deposition. Why? For several possible reasons:

1. At the time of the taking of your deposition, the opposing lawyer may have been of the opinion that there are weaknesses to your position which he or she would prefer not bringing to your attention (or to your lawyer's attention). The idea is to place you in a more difficult position in responding, i.e., placing you in a position of being caught off guard.

2. Since the taking of your deposition, important information may have come to the attention of the opposing lawyer which was not available at the time of the deposition.

3. Frequently, the lawyer is better prepared to question you at trial than he or she was at the time of your deposition.

If any of these situations arise, there is no cause for undue concern. Usually, your lawyer will have anticipated any such questions and advised you how best to respond. In any event, treat the question as you would any other. And, in responding, follow the previous suggestions on deposition testimony in chapter 5.

When a trial takes place months or years after an event it is easy to forget many of the details of what happened. Sometimes you may recall an event differently at a trial than you did at a deposition a year earlier. When you say something at trial that is different from what you said at a deposition, the opposing lawyer may point it out to the judge or jury and claim that you are, or were, lying. Such differences may damage your case unless there is a logical explanation for the difference in your testimony.

As previously noted, prior to trial you should carefully review your earlier deposition testimony to refresh your memory.

If you testify and are cross-examined, do not allow the opposing lawyer to incorrectly suggest that there is a discrepancy between your trial testimony on a particular point and your deposition testimony when there is no such discrepancy. In law, showing such a discrepancy is known as *impeachment*. The term impeachment means that the opposing lawyer is attempting to suggest that your testimony at trial is not credible because it differs, in an important way, from your deposition testimony (or some other previous statement). If it does differ, that is a fact you will have to accept, and offer whatever explanation you have. If it does not differ, you should not permit the opposing lawyer to suggest that it does.

On this point, you should not rely totally on your lawyer. True, if the opposing counsel is intending to suggest a discrepancy which is not well-founded, your lawyer will no doubt object, and the apparent damage may be undone. However, trials are usually fast paced, and it may be difficult for your lawyer to timely intervene. At trial you should be able to determine for yourself whether your trial testimony differs from that given at deposition. If it does not, and your lawyer does not protect you on the point, protect yourself. If possible, point out to the lawyer that your trial testimony is not, in fact, inconsistent with your deposition testimony (or some other statement) and why it is not.

Your Conduct During Trial

From the beginning to the end of the trial process, observe these rules:

- Other than a "good morning," "good afternoon," or "good evening," do not speak to prospective jurors or to jurors who have been selected for your jury. Why? Because it is inappropriate and could be extremely damaging to your case.

- Other than a form of greeting, do not engage in "friendly conversation" with the opposing lawyer, your opponent, or any key witnesses for your opponent. If observed by a member of the jury (or a prospective juror), that juror may incorrectly conclude that you do not view your case as a serious one; otherwise, you would not be engaging in what might appear to be friendly conversation with your opponents.

- Whenever in view of a juror (or a possible juror), maintain a calm, serious, dignified manner. For example, do not engage in "light-hearted" or joking conversation with anyone. Again, your case is a serious matter; otherwise, you would not be in the courtroom. If it appears to a juror that you are not serious about your case, they may conclude there is no reason for them to consider it seriously and act accordingly.

- Unless you are testifying, do not make any statement in the presence of the jury (or a juror).

- Whenever a witness is testifying, do not express your view of that testimony by facial expressions, utterances, or any other conduct. Such conduct is inappropriate and could be viewed by the jury to your disadvantage.

☞ Remember at all times that as a practical matter and in varying degrees, depending on the case, *you* are on trial, that is, in many cases, whether you win or lose your case can depend on how you (and your credibility) are viewed by the fact-finder.

☞ Above all, throughout the trial process, maintain your composure. Why? For three reasons:

1. If you lose your composure and the question of your credibility is at issue, the fact-finder may conclude that your testimony is not credible; and your claim or defense is without merit for that reason.

2. By losing your composure, you will have diminished your ability to assist your lawyer in winning your case (i.e., if you are angry, you cannot think rationally).

3. If you do not lose your composure, even under the strongest provocation, you may increase your credibility in the view of the fact-finder.

POST-TRIAL AND PRE-APPEAL PROCEEDINGS

7

POST-TRIAL MOTIONS

After the jury has returned its verdict (or, in a non-jury trial, the court has announced its decision), either your lawyer or the lawyer for your opponent may file certain post-trial motions depending on the outcome of the case. For example, the losing party may file a *motion for new trial*. Such a motion can be based on a variety of grounds, including insufficiency of the evidence to support the verdict, legal irregularities which occurred during the trial, etc. If the jury (or the court in a non-jury trial) awarded damages, the losing party may file a motion seeking to have the court reduce the amount of damages awarded.

Generally, a hearing will be held before the court on any such motions, during which the lawyers for the respective parties will be allowed the opportunity to be heard on the merits of the motions. Such motions and proceedings usually raise purely technical, legal matters, and, for that reason, you may be unable to help your lawyer on the subject. However, this is not always the case.

How You Can Help in Post-Trial Motions

In some cases, motions for new trial or to reduce an award for damages raise factual issues. Obviously, you may be in a position to assist your lawyer with respect to factual issues by:

1. Making certain that the factual matters presented by such motions are presented accurately.

2. Assuring that the factual presentation is complete, i.e., that facts which may be important to a particular issue involved are not omitted.

Of course, it is the responsibility of your lawyer to assure that both of these objectives are met. However, if you can assist in this regard, do so.

PRE-APPEAL PROCEEDINGS

During post-trial/pre-appeal proceedings, there are two subjects or events with which you may be directly involved. First, the question of an appeal. In most cases, and in most states, the losing party has a right to appeal the judgment rendered to an appropriate appellate court. That fact does not mean that the losing party must take an appeal, but rather, only that the appellate process is available to the losing party if they desire to use it. If you are the losing party, you will make that decision after consulting with your lawyer. That consultation should include a discussion of two subjects: your lawyer's opinion as to your likelihood of success, and the cost of pursuing the appeal.

Ask for your lawyer's advice as to your relative chances for success on appeal. Unfortunately, for a variety of reasons, your lawyer may not be in a position to provide you with concrete or definitive advice on this subject. However, your lawyer should be in a position to at least provide you with a general, broad range of estimates for success on appeal. For example, in most instances, the lawyer should be able to advise you (although not guarantee) as to whether you have little chance of success, a fifty percent chance of success, or a better than fifty percent chance of success.

Also consider what an appeal will cost. If your fee arrangement with your lawyer does not include attorneys' fees and costs in taking an appeal, you will be obligated to pay additional attorneys' fees and costs in order to appeal. (If your fee arrangement is a contingent one, fees in processing an appeal are usually agreed to in that agreement.) Ask your lawyer's advice as to the amount of fees and costs which he or she estimates you will be required to expend in order to appeal.

The word "estimate" is used since fees and costs can vary widely depending on a number of circumstances. For example, some lawyers may require a fixed fee, while others may base the fee on an hourly rate. Similarly, the court costs involved will vary from case to case, largely depending on the length of the trial. Your lawyer should be in a position to give you guidance on these subjects, and you should certainly seek it before determining whether to take an appeal. Obviously, if you will incur a substantial, additional expense in order to take an appeal, you may choose not to do so if your chances for success on appeal are limited to a significant degree.

Alternatively, even if you are advised by your lawyer that your chances for success on appeal are relatively good, you may not be in a financial position to take the appeal, i.e., you are not in a position to pay additional fees and costs. In some instances, if you are successful on appeal, either a part or all of these additional fees and costs may be awardable against your opponent. However, such awards are subject to the same qualifications previously discussed with respect to the collectibility of judgments. Your lawyer should be in a position to provide you some guidance on this issue.

Finally, your lawyer may limit his or her legal practice to trials only; therefore, they do not handle appeals. In that instance, your lawyer will make you aware of that fact, and will no doubt assist you (if you require assistance) in retaining another lawyer to handle the appeal. In deciding whether you wish to make an appeal, or resist an appeal, you will wish to include in your consideration those factors previously discussed in connection withthe issue of what it means to win (as discussed on page 8).

SETTLEMENT NEGOTIATIONS

Another subject or event may arise in the post-trial/pre-appeal stage which will require your direct involvement: the possibility of a settlement. For example, if you are the winning party in the trial court and the losing party intends to take an appeal, they may attempt to negotiate a settlement before doing so in order to avoid the necessity of an appeal. Similarly, even if the opposing party does not attempt to initiate settlement negotiations at that stage, it may be to your advantage to attempt to negotiate a settlement.

You may say why, if I am the winning party, and the verdict or judgment is in my favor, would I wish to consider the possibility of negotiating a settlement in order to avoid an appeal? There are three potential reasons:

1. To avoid additional expenses which may not be recoverable from the other party.
2. To eliminate further delay in resolving the case.
3. To avoid the possibility that the appellate court might reverse the verdict or judgment in the lower court.

Your lawyer should be in a position to give you specific guidance on these subjects. Similarly, if you are the losing party, you should discuss with your lawyer the possibility of attempting to negotiate a settlement in order to avoid an appeal. Again, he or she should be in a position to give you guidance. Whether you are the winning party or the losing party, there will be a variety of factors which your lawyer will no doubt suggest you consider in making this decision.

If you choose to take an appeal, in some instances (usually infrequent), you may be in a position to assist your lawyer in determining what points or arguments should be raised on appeal. Usually, this subject is a highly technical one which can only be determined by your lawyer. If your lawyer either does not handle appeals, or has limited experience in that field of practice, another lawyer who specializes in appeals will determine the point or points. In any event, at least ask your lawyer whether your assistance might be helpful, and, if so, provide it.

APPEALS

THE APPEAL PROCESS

While the legal technicalities which may apply to appeals vary in some degree from state to state and in the federal appellate system, the basic structure of the appeal process is substantially similar regardless of the state or federal court involved. An *appeal* is simply a method by which one who is a party to an action in a trial court, and who is dissatisfied with the result reached in a trial court, may seek a review of that result by another court (an *appellate* court).

There are numerous and varied grounds which are legally recognized as a basis for seeking such review (*taking an appeal*, or *appealing*). These grounds are beyond the scope of this book, since you need not be aware of them in order to help your lawyer during the appeal process. In an appeal based on any one or more of these recognized grounds, the appealing party (usually referred to as the *appellant*) will attempt to persuade the appellate court that the result reached in the trial court was wrong or erroneous, and should be set aside (*reversed* or *overturned*) or modified in some way. The party opposing the appeal (usually referred to as the *appellee*) will attempt to persuade the appellate court that the result reached in the trial court was correct and should be allowed to stand (*affirmed*).

In practice, usually the appellant will file with the appellate court a written statement (a *brief*) setting forth the grounds and arguments for the appeal. The appellee then has the opportunity to file a brief in response. Frequently, the appellant may be permitted to file a further brief in response to that filed by the appellee. In many cases, the appellant and appellee are then allowed to supplement or add to their written briefs by an oral presentation to the court, through an *oral argument*.

After all briefs have been submitted and oral arguments heard, the court, based on the briefs and argument, will decide what action, if any, it wishes to take on the appeal and issue its *decision* or *opinion* (which is usually in writing). In that decision or opinion, the court may set aside (reverse the result in the trial court, let that result stand (affirm), or modify it in some way.

In some cases, the party who is dissatisfied with the decision may seek to have the court reconsider, by filing a *motion for rehearing*. If such a motion is filed, the opposing party will be allowed to respond. The court will rule on the motion, either granting or denying it. If the motion is granted, the court may allow additional briefs or argument. If the court decides to *rehear* the appeal, it may re-affirm its prior decision, reverse it, or modify it in some way. In most cases, the appellate process is now at an end. If the court reverses the result reached in the trial court (or, in some cases, modifies it), the case will be returned to the trial court, for further action. That further action may (but not always) require that the case be re-tried, in which event the trial process begins anew.

Because an appellate court has the power to set aside a result reached in the trial court, it is obvious that, if an appeal is taken in your case, either by you or your opponent, the event is an extremely important one.

HOW YOU CAN HELP WITH THE APPEAL

Most of the appellate process involves quite technical, legal matters as to which you will most probably not be in a position to assist your lawyer. However, there are two areas in that process in which you might wish to participate, and offer your help.

Briefs

Briefs filed in an appeal are usually divided into two parts:

1. A discussion of those *facts* established by the evidence in the trial court which the parties argue or contend are important to deciding the issues raised in the appeal.

2. A discussion of the *legal principles* and *authorities* the parties argue or contend should be applied to those facts.

In some cases, the appeal may raise only technical, procedural issues in which the facts established in the trial court are of little or no importance.

If an appeal in your case will raise issues which require a consideration of facts established in the trial court, a *record* will be made a part of the appeal proceedings. In part, this record will consist of a written transcript of all hearings in the trial court at which witnesses testified or documentary evidence was considered, including the trial itself. That record will be sent to the appellate court so that it will have it for reference when considering the briefs of the parties when they are filed (and at oral argument if one is held).

The preparation of an appellate brief can be quite complex, and require considerable legal skill and experience. Obviously, the legal aspects of preparing such briefs are beyond the scope of this book. However, certain aspects of the mechanics involved in preparing a brief which will discuss the facts established in the trial court can be important to you.

In preparing such a brief (or briefs), your lawyer will analyze (among other things) the transcript of the trial (and any other important proceedings which were transcribed) and locate where in the transcript the facts important to the issues raised on the appeal are cited. These facts will include not only those which your lawyer believes support your position on the issues raised on appeal, but also those which your opponent's lawyer argues in his or her brief (or briefs) support your opponent's position on the issues raised.

The task of locating where in the transcript these facts appear is necessary because any reference to them in the briefs must contain a notation identifying the pages, by number, in the transcript where they appear. Thus, the appellate court, and the lawyer for the opposing party, can check the reference for accuracy. If the transcript involved is lengthy, this task can be time-consuming. Perhaps, you can help. Ask your lawyer if you can be of assistance by:

☞ Locating in the transcript the facts your lawyer believes are important to your position on the issues raised.

☞ Locating in the transcript the facts referred to by your opponent's lawyer in their brief (or briefs), and checking them for accuracy.

☞ Checking the accuracy of all references in drafts of your lawyer's brief (or briefs) to facts in the transcript.

If your lawyer accepts your offer to assist in one or more of these ways, in checking for accuracy, you will be checking: (a) the accuracy of the facts referred to in the brief against the facts as they appear in the transcript; and (b) the accuracy of the notation in the brief to page numbers in the transcript. The task of checking the accuracy of references to facts in briefs is extremely important for two reasons:

1. An error in your brief (or briefs) which misstates an important fact can seriously reduce your chances for success; and

2. The failure to point out to the appellate court an error of fact which appears in your opponent's brief (or briefs) can likewise reduce your chances for success.

So, if your lawyer accepts your offer to assist in these ways, you can not only act as a safeguard for accuracy, but also reduce the amount of time your lawyer (or a paralegal) may be required to spend on briefs, thereby perhaps reducing fees.

When the court issues a decision, you may have two additional opportunities to assist your lawyer in checking for accuracy. In many cases (particularly where the court reverses the result reached in the trial court), the written decision of the court will refer to, and rely on, factual matters in the transcript or other parts of the record. These references must be checked for accuracy as well. In addition, if a motion for rehearing on the decision is filed and refers to factual matters, those references must be checked for accuracy as well.

Oral Argument

If the appellate court permits oral argument, you may also be able to assist your lawyer at the argument.

First, ask your lawyer if you should attend the oral argument. For a variety of reasons, your lawyer may advise either that you should, or should not, attend. Of course, you have an absolute right to attend if you wish, but I suggest you leave this decision to your lawyer. If your lawyer suggests that you do attend, by all means, do so. Aside from other reasons a lawyer might offer for the advisability of your attendance, you may be able to assist the lawyer in the actual oral presentation to be made.

For example, many lawyers experienced in appeals wish to have someone accompany them to the oral argument, whether it be a law partner, an associate in a law firm, a secretary, or the client. This is for the purpose of assuring that accurate notes are made during the presentation of specific points and arguments made by the lawyer for your opponent, and more importantly, questions or comments which may be asked or made by judges of the appellate court during the presentation.

At oral arguments, members of the court frequently ask the respective lawyers questions or make comments. In many instances, the exact question asked or comments made could be very important. Moreover, responses of the lawyers to questions by the court can be significant. Obviously, while your lawyer is making his or her oral presentation, and a question is asked or comment made by a member of the court during that presentation, it may be quite difficult for the lawyer to make accurate notes of such questions or comments at the time (although the lawyer will attempt to do so). The same is true with points or arguments made by opposing counsel. Having accurate notes of these matters can be of great assistance to your lawyer for use later in the argument. Moreover, these notes may be important after arguments are concluded, in connection with a motion for rehearing.

No one may be available from your lawyer's office to fulfill this function. Alternatively, someone may be available, but at an added cost to you. So, ask your lawyer if you can assist by taking notes.

Also, if there are numerous documents which may be referred to during the argument, you may be in a position to assist by organizing them for your lawyer, and, during the argument, assisting your lawyer in locating specific documents at appropriate times.

Finally, during oral argument a question may arise as to a factual matter contained in the record on appeal. If so, you may assist your lawyer in locating the appropriate reference in the record.

Appendix A
Checklists

The checklists on the following pages will help you prepare for various stages of your case.

Checklist 1
Preparation for Initial Meeting

❏ Written narrative?

❏ Date, time, place

❏ What happened

❏ Oral conversations

❏ Persons present

❏ Persons with whom discussed

❏ Persons with whom opponent discussed

❏ Writings prepared by you

❏ Writings prepared by opponent

❏ Writings prepared by third-parties

❏ Other persons having knowledge

❏ Reputation ("character") witnesses (yours)

❏ Reputation ("character") witnesses (your opponent's)

❏ Photographs

❏ Videotapes

❏ Audiotapes

❏ Amount of monies claimed

❏ Persons having knowledge of monies claimed

❏ Writings regarding monies claimed

❏ Nature of injuries

❏ Persons having knowledge of injuries

❏ Past medical history

❏ Medical reports, bills, etc.

❏ Persons who will dispute your version

❏ Date, time, place of prior discussions; who present; what said

❏ Technical matters; specialized matters

❏ Opponent's involvement with third parties

❏ Media coverage (your claim/defense)

❏ Media coverage (related matter)

❏ Electronic recordings without consent

❏ Prior criminal record

❏ Prior criminal record of opponent

❏ Prior criminal record of key witnesses

❏ Prior/pending litigation

❏ Written/oral prior inconsistent statements

❏ Accurate addresses, telephone numbers

❏ Travel plans of witnesses

❏ Health problems of witnesses

❏ Provide all writings/physical objects; inventory

Checklist 2
What to Discuss/Ask at Initial Meeting

❏ Provide information gathered during preparation

❏ Additional information needed?

❏ Written narrative?

❏ Clear and concise; chronological order

❏ Unimportant facts

❏ Facts vs. Guesses

❏ Emotions

❏ Present documents

❏ Documents in possession of third parties

❏ Date of claim

❏ How damaged

❏ Claims against opponent

❏ Claims against co-defendants

❏ Claims against third parties

❏ "Undermining" documents

❏ Chances of success

❏ "Exposure"

❏ Compromise/settlement

❏ Types of damages

❏ Factual elements of claims/defenses

❏ Discussions with third parties

❏ Conflicts

❏ Jury vs. Non-jury trial

- ❏ "Expert" witnesses
- ❏ Collectibility
- ❏ Litigation alternatives
- ❏ Basis of fee arrangement
- ❏ Written fee agreement
- ❏ Review of information provided; corrections?; additions?
- ❏ Digest advice given; questions?

Checklist 3
Discovery

- ❏ "Theory of case"
- ❏ How you can help?
- ❏ Update witnesses, writings
- ❏ Additional investigation?
- ❏ Inaccurate, incomplete, misleading information?
- ❏ Answers to interrogatories
- ❏ Requests for production of documents; responding
- ❏ Review pleadings of opponent for accuracy
- ❏ Outline of points to include at depositions
- ❏ Interviewing key witnesses
- ❏ Searching for documents
- ❏ Photographs
- ❏ Drafting requests for product of documents
- ❏ Drafting subpoenas for documents
- ❏ Reviewing compliance with requests for production of documents/subpoenas
- ❏ Continuances; extensions of time
- ❏ Stipulations
- ❏ Opponent's "Theory of case"
- ❏ Preparing for your deposition
- ❏ Answering questions at deposition
- ❏ Summary judgment

Checklist 4
Trial

❏ Jury selection

❏ Organizing documents

❏ Factual points to be made at trial

❏ Questioning of witnesses at trial

❏ Conduct in presence of jurors

❏ Conduct while testifying

❏ Matters raised for first time at trial

❏ Prior inconsistent statements of witnesses

❏ Notes of testimony

❏ Maintaining your composure

❏ Prior inconsistent statements of your own

Appendix B
Information Forms

The forms on the following pages should be filled out before your initial meeting with your lawyer. Copies can be given to your lawyer to save him or her (and you) money in locating witnesses and documents.

Witnesses

Name:
Address(es):
Telephone number(s):
Expected testimony:
Possession of Documents:
❏ Friendly   ❏ Hostile
Name:
Address(es):
Telephone number(s):
Expected testimony:
Possession of Documents:
❏ Friendly   ❏ Hostile

Witnesses

Name:

Address(es):

Telephone number(s):

Expected testimony:

Possession of Documents:

❏ Friendly   ❏ Hostile

Name:

Address(es):

Telephone number(s):

Expected testimony:

Possession of Documents:

❏ Friendly   ❏ Hostile

Witnesses

Name:
Address(es):
Telephone number(s):
Expected testimony:
Possession of Documents:
❑ Friendly ❑ Hostile

Name:
Address(es):
Telephone number(s):
Expected testimony:
Possession of Documents:
❑ Friendly ❑ Hostile

Witnesses

Name:

Address(es):

Telephone number(s):

Expected testimony:

Possession of Documents:

❏ Friendly   ❏ Hostile

Name:

Address(es):

Telephone number(s):

Expected testimony:

Possession of Documents:

❏ Friendly   ❏ Hostile

Documents

Description:

Contents:

Location/Possession of Original (name, address, phone):

Location/Possession of Copies (name, address, phone):

Person(s) with knowledge of (name, address, phone):

Description:

Contents:

Location/Possession of Original (name, address, phone):

Location/Possession of Copies (name, address, phone):

Person(s) with knowledge of (name, address, phone):

Documents

Description:

Contents:

Location/Possession of Original (name, address, phone):

Location/Possession of Copies (name, address, phone):

Person(s) with knowledge of (name, address, phone):

Description:

Contents:

Location/Possession of Original (name, address, phone):

Location/Possession of Copies (name, address, phone):

Person(s) with knowledge of (name, address, phone):

Documents

Description:

Contents:

Location/Possession of Original (name, address, phone):

Location/Possession of Copies (name, address, phone):

Person(s) with knowledge of (name, address, phone):

Description:

Contents:

Location/Possession of Original (name, address, phone):

Location/Possession of Copies (name, address, phone):

Person(s) with knowledge of (name, address, phone):

Documents

Description:

Contents:

Location/Possession of Original (name, address, phone):

Location/Possession of Copies (name, address, phone):

Person(s) with knowledge of (name, address, phone):

Description:

Contents:

Location/Possession of Original (name, address, phone):

Location/Possession of Copies (name, address, phone):

Person(s) with knowledge of (name, address, phone):

APPENDIX C
LAWYER REFERRAL
INFORMATION

This appendix contains a list of addresses and telephone numbers for state bar associations and other national lawyer groups, to serve as a starting point for lawyer referrals. There are many referral services, offered by both local bar associations and private referral companies. Those listed in this appendix may be able to provide you with a local referral service, and you may also want to check with your local county or city bar association, or the Yellow Pages of your telephone directory under the headings *Attorney Referral Services* or *Attorneys*.

State Bar Associations

AL: Alabama State Bar
415 Dexter St.
Montgomery, AL 36104
205-269-1515

AK: Alaska Bar Association
P.O. Box 100279
Anchorage, AK 99510
907-272-7469

AZ: State Bar of Arizona
363 N 1st Ave.
Phoenix, AZ 85003
602-252-4804

AR: Arkansas Bar Association
400 W. Markham St.
Little Rock, AR 72201
501-375-4605

CA: State Bar of California
555 Franklin St.
San Francisco, CA 94102
415-561-8200

CO: Colorado Bar Association
1900 Grant St., Ste. 950
Denver, CO 80203
303-860-1112

CT: Connecticut Bar Association
101 Corporate Pl.
Rocky Hill, CT 06067
203-721-0025

DE: Delaware State Bar Association
1225 King St.
Wilmington, DE 19801
302-658-5279

DC: District of Columbia Bar Association
1250 H St. NW, 6th Fl
Washington, DC 20005
202-737-4700

FL: Florida Bar
650 Apalachee Pkwy.
Tallahassee, FL 32399
904-561-5600

GA: State Bar of Georgia
50 Hurt Plaza, Hurt Bldg. Ste. 800
Atlanta, GA 30303
404-527-8700

HI: Hawaii State Bar
1136 Union Mall, PH 1
Honolulu, HI 96813
808-537-1868

ID: Idaho State Bar
PO Box 895
Boise, ID 83701
208-342-8958

IL: Illinois State Bar Association
424 S. 2nd St.
Springfield, IL 62701
217-525-1760

IN: Indiana State Bar Association
230 E. Ohio St. 4th Fl
Indianapolis, IN 46204
317-639-5465

IA: Iowa State Bar Association
521 E. Locust
Des Moines, IA 50309
515-243-3179

KS: Kansas Bar Association
P.O. Box 1037
Topeka, KS 66601
913-234-5696

KY: Kentucky Bar Association
514 W. Main St.
Frankfort, KY 40601
502-564-3795

LA: Louisiana State Bar Association
601 St. Charles Ave.
New Orleans, LA 70130
504-566-1600

ME: Maine State Bar Association
124 State St.
Augusta, ME 04330
207-622-7523

MD: Maryland State Bar Association
      520 W. Fayette St.
      Baltimore, MD 21201
      410-685-7878

MA: Massachusetts bar Association
      20 West St.
      Boston, MA 02111
      617-542-3602

MI: State Bar of Michigan
      306 Townsend St.
      Lansing, MI 48933
      517-372-9030

MN: Minnesota State Bar Association
      514 Nicollett Mall, Ste. 300
      Minneapolis, MN 55402
      612-333-1183

MS: Mississippi State Bar Association
      643 N. State St.
      Jackson, MS 39202
      601-948-4471

MO: Missouri Bar
      326 Monroe St.
      Jefferson City, MO 65101
      314-635-4128

MT: State Bar of Montana
      46 N Last Chance Gulch St., Ste. 2A
      Helena, MT 59601
      406-442-7660

NE: Nebraska State Bar Association
        P.O. Box 81809
        Lincoln, NE 68501
        402-475-7091

NV: State Bar of Nevada
        201 Las Vegas Blvd. S., Ste. 200
        Las Vegas, NV 89101
        702-382-2200

NH: New Hampshire Bar Association
        112 Pleasant St.
        Concord, NH 03301
        603-224-6942

NJ: New Jersey State Bar Association
        1 Constitution Square
        New Brunswick, NJ 08901
        908-249-5000

NM: State Bar of New Mexico
        121 Tierras Ave. NE
        Albuquerque, NM 87102
        505-842-6132

NY: New York State Bar Association
        1 Elk St.
        Albany, NY 12207
        518-463-3200

NC: North Carolina State Bar
        PO Box 25908
        Raleigh, NC 27611
        919-828-4620

ND: State Bar Association of North Dakota
515 1/2 E. Broadway Ave., Ste. 101
Bismarck, ND 58501
701-255-1404

OH: Ohio State Bar Association
Lake Shore Dr.
Columbus, OH 43204
614-487-2050

OK: Oklahoma Bar Association
1901 N. Lincoln Blvd.
Oklahoma City, OK 73105
405-524-2365

OR: Oregon State Bar Association
5200 SW Meadows Rd.
Lake Oswego, OR 97035
503-620-0222

PA: Pennsylvania Bar Association
100 South St.
Harrisburg, PA 17101
717-238-6715

PR: Puerto Rico Bar Association
Apartados 1900
San Juan, PR 00903
809-721-3358

RI: Rhode Island Bar Association
115 Cedar St.
Providence, RI 02903
401-421-5740

SC: South Carolina Bar
PO Box 608
Columbia, SC 29202
803-799-6653

SD: State Bar of South Dakota
222 E. Capitol Ave.
Pierre, SD 57501
605-224-7554

TN: Tennessee Bar Association
3622 West End Ave.
Nashville, TN 37205
615-383-7421

TX: State Bar of Texas
1414 Colorado St.
Austin, TX 78701
512-463-1400

UT: Utah State Bar Association
645 South 200 East, Ste. 310
Salt Lake City, UT 84111
801-531-9077

VT: Vermont Bar Association
P.O. Box 100
Montpelier, VT 05601
802-223-2020

VA: Virginia State Bar
707 E. Main St., Ste. 1500
Richmond, VA 23219
804-775-0500

WA: Washington State Bar
      2001 6th Ave., Westin Bldg. Ste. 500
      Seattle, WA 98121
      206-727-8200

WV: West Virginia State Bar
      2006 Kanawha Blvd. E.
      Charleston, WV 25311
      304-558-2456

WI: State Bar of Wisconsin
      402 W. Wilson St.
      Madison, WI 53703
      608-257-3838

WY: Wyoming State Bar
      P.O. Box 109
      Cheyenne, WY 82003
      307-632-9061

National Organizations

Environmental Law Institute
1616 P St. NW, 2nd Fl
Washington, DC 20036
202-328-5150

Federal Bar Association
1815 H St. NW, Ste. 408
Washington, DC 20006
202-638-0252

International Association of Defense Counsel
20 N Wacker Dr., Ste. 3100
Chicago, IL 60606
312-368-1494

National Council of Juvenile & Family Court Judges
1041 N. Virginia St., 3rd Fl
Reno, NV 89557
702-784-6012

National Institute of Municipal Law Officers
1000 Connecticut Ave. NW, Ste. 902
Washington, DC 20036
202-466-5424

National Legal Aid & Defender Association
1625 K St. NW, 8th Fl
Washington, DC 20006
202-452-0620

Practicing Law Institute
810 7th Ave., 29th Fl
New York, NY 10019
212-765-5700

Vera Institute of Justice
377 Broadway
New York, NY 10013
212-334-1300

INDEX

Your #1 Source for Real World Legal Information...

Sphinx® Publishing

• Written by lawyers • Simple English explanation of the law
• Forms and instructions included

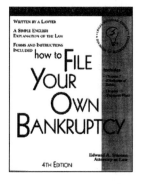

How to File Your Own Bankruptcy
(or How to Avoid It), 4th Ed.

Whether you are considering filing for bankruptcy or are looking
to avoid it at all costs, this book
can help you. Includes instructions and forms and more!

208 pages; $19.95;
ISBN 1-57071-223-9

Defend Yourself against Criminal
Charges

Aids consumers in understanding the
criminal justice system and explains
their rights in regards to searches,
arrests, and police questioning.

192 pages; $19.95;
ISBN 1-57071-162-3

What our customers say about our books:

"It couldn't be more clear for the layperson." —R.D.

"I want you to know I really appreciate your book. It has saved me a lot of time
and money." —L.T.

"Your real estate contracts book has saved me nearly $12,000.00 in closing costs
over the past year." —A.B.

"...many of the legal questions that I have had over the years were answered clearly
and concisely through your plain English interpretation of the law." —C.E.H.

"If there weren't people out there like you I'd be lost. You have the best books of
this type out there." —S.B.

"...your forms and directions are easy to follow." —C.V.M.

*Sphinx Publishing's Legal Survival Guides are directly available from the publisher,
or from your local bookstores.*

*For credit card orders call 1–800–43–BRIGHT,
write P.O. Box 4410, Naperville, IL 60567-4410, or fax 630-961-2168*

SPHINX® PUBLISHING'S STATE TITLES
Up-to-date for Your State

CALIFORNIA

CA Power of Attorney Handbook	$12.95
How to File for Divorce in CA	$19.95
How to Make a CA Will	$12.95
How to Probate an Estate in CA	$19.95
How to Start a Business in CA	$16.95
How to Win in Small Claims Court in CA	$14.95
Landlords' Rights and Duties in CA	$19.95

FLORIDA

Florida Power of Attorney Handbook (2E)	$12.95
How to File for Divorce in FL (6E)	$21.95
How to Form a Limited Liability Company in FL	$19.95
How to Form a Nonprofit Corp in FL (3E)	$19.95
How to Form a Corporation in FL (4E)	$19.95
How to Form a Partnership in FL	$19.95
How to Make a FL Will (6E)	$12.95
How to Modify Your FL Divorce Judgement (4E)	$22.95
How to Probate an Estate in FL (3E)	$24.95
How to Start a Business in FL (5E)	$16.95
How to Win in Small Claims Court in FL (6E)	$14.95
Land Trusts in FL (5E)	$24.95
Landlords' Rights and Duties in FL (7E)	$19.95
Women's Legal Rights in FL	$19.95

GEORGIA

How to File for Divorce in GA (3E)	$19.95
How to Make a GA Will (3E)	$12.95
How to Start a Business in GA (3E)	$16.95

ILLINOIS

How to File for Divorce in IL (2E)	$19.95
How to Make an IL Will (2E)	$12.95
How to Start a Business in IL (2E)	$16.95
Landlords' Rights & Duties in IL	$19.95

MASSACHUSETTS

How to File for Divorce in MA (2E)	$19.95
How to Make a MA Will (2E)	$9.95
How to Probate an Estate in MA (2E)	$19.95
How to Start a Business in MA (2E)	$16.95
Landlords' Rights and Duties in MA (2E)	$19.95

Sphinx Publishing's Legal Survival Guides are directly available from the publisher, or from your local bookstores.

MICHIGAN

How to File for Divorce in MI (2E)	$19.95
How to Make a MI Will (2E)	$12.95
How to Start a Business in MI (2E)	$16.95

MINNESOTA

How to File for Divorce in MN	$19.95
How to Form a Simple Corporation in MN	$19.95
How to Make a MN Will	$9.95
How to Start a Business in MN	$16.95

NEW YORK

How to File for Divorce in NY	$19.95
How to Form a Corporation in NY	$19.95
How to Make a NY Will (2E)	$12.95
How to Start a Business in NY	$16.95
How to Win in Small Claims Court in NY	$14.95
Landlords' Rights and Duties in NY	$19.95
New York Power of Attorney Handbook	$19.95

NORTH CAROLINA

How to File for Divorce in NC (2E)	$19.95
How to Make a NC Will (2E)	$12.95
How to Start a Business in NC (2E)	$16.95
Landlords' Rights & Duties in NC	$19.95

OHIO

How to File for Divorce in OH	$19.95

PENNSYLVANIA

How to File for Divorce in PA	$19.95
How to Make a PA Will (2E)	$12.95
How to Start a Business in PA (2E)	$16.95
Landlords' Rights and Duties in PA	$19.95

TEXAS

How to File for Divorce in TX (2E)	$19.95
How to Form a Simple Corporation in TX	$19.95
How to Make a TX Will (2E)	$12.95
How to Probate an Estate in TX (2E)	$19.95
How to Start a Business in TX (2E)	$16.95
How to Win in Small Claims Court in TX (2E)	$14.95
Landlords' Rights and Duties in TX (2E)	$19.95

For credit card orders call 1–800–43–BRIGHT,
write P.O. Box 4410, Naperville, IL 60567-4410, or fax 630-961-2168

SPHINX® PUBLISHING'S NATIONAL TITLES
Valid in All 50 States

LEGAL SURVIVAL IN BUSINESS

How to Form a Limited Liability Company	$19.95
How to Form a DE Corporation from Any State	$19.95
How to Form a NV Corporation from Any State	$19.95
How to Form a Nonprofit Corporation	$24.95
How to Form Your Own Corporation (2E)	$19.95
How to Form Your Own Partnership	$19.95
How to Register Your Own Copyright (2E)	$19.95
How to Register Your Own Trademark (3E)	$19.95
Most Valuable Business Legal Forms You'll Ever Need (2E)	$19.95
Most Valuable Corporate Forms You'll Ever Need (2E)	$24.95
Software Law (with diskette)	$29.95

LEGAL SURVIVAL IN COURT

Crime Victim's Guide to Justice	$19.95
Debtors' Rights (3E)	$12.95
Defend Yourself against Criminal Charges	$19.95
Grandparents' Rights (2E)	$19.95
Help Your Lawyer Win Your Case (2E)	$12.95
How to Win Your Unemployment Compensation Claim	$19.95
Jurors' Rights (2E)	$9.95
Legal Malpractice and Other Claims	$18.95
Legal Research Made Easy (2E)	$14.95
Your Right to Child Custody, Support and Visitation	$19.95
Simple Ways to Protect Yourself from Lawsuits	$24.95
Unmarried Parents' Rights	$19.95
Victim's Rights	$12.95
Winning Your Personal Injury Claim	$19.95

LEGAL SURVIVAL IN REAL ESTATE

How to Buy a Condominium or Townhome	$16.95
How to Negotiate Real Estate Contracts (3E)	$16.95
How to Negotiate Real Estate Leases (3E)	$16.95
Successful Real Estate Brokerage Management	$19.95

LEGAL SURVIVAL IN PERSONAL AFFAIRS

How to File Your Own Bankruptcy (4E)	$19.95
How to File Your Own Divorce (3E)	$19.95
How to Make Your Own Will	$12.95
How to Write Your Own Living Will	$9.95
How to Write Your Own Premarital Agreement (2E)	$19.95
Living Trusts and Simple Ways to Avoid Probate (2E)	$19.95
Most Valuable Personal Legal Forms You'll Ever Need	$14.95
The Nanny and Domestic Legal Help Kit	$19.95
Neighbor vs. Neighbor	$12.95
The Power of Attorney Handbook (3E)	$19.95
Social Security Benefits Handbook (2E)	$14.95
Unmarried Parents' Rights	$19.95
U.S.A. Immigration Guide (3E)	$19.95
Guía de Inmigración a Estados Unidos (2E)	$19.95

SPHINX® PUBLISHING ORDER FORM

BILL TO:			SHIP TO:		

Phone #	Terms	F.O.B.	Chicago, IL	Ship Date

Charge my: ☐ VISA   ☐ MasterCard   ☐ American Express   ☐ **Money Order or Personal Check**

Credit Card Number   **Expiration Date**

Qty	ISBN	Title	Retail
	SPHINX PUBLISHING NATIONAL TITLES		
____	1-57071-166-6	Crime Victim's Guide to Justice	$19.95
____	1-57071-342-1	Debtors' Rights (3E)	$12.95
____	1-57071-162-3	Defend Yourself against Criminal Charges	$19.95
____	1-57248-082-3	Grandparents' Rights (2E)	$19.95
____	1-57248-087-4	Guia de Inmigracion a Estados Unidos (2E)	$19.95
____	1-57248-103-X	Help Your Lawyer Win Your Case (2E)	$12.95
____	1-57071-164-X	How to Buy a Condominium or Townhome	$16.95
____	1-57071-223-9	How to File Your Own Bankruptcy (4E)	$19.95
____	1-57071-224-7	How to File Your Own Divorce (3E)	$19.95
____	1-57248-083-1	How to Form a Limited Liability Company	$19.95
____	1-57248-100-5	How to Form a DE Corporation from Any State	$19.95
____	1-57248-101-3	How to Form a NV Corporation from Any State	$19.95
____	1-57248-099-8	How to Form a Nonprofit Corporation	$24.95
____	1-57071-227-1	How to Form Your Own Corporation (2E)	$19.95
____	1-57071-343-X	How to Form Your Own Partnership	$19.95
____	1-57071-228-X	How to Make Your Own Will	$12.95
____	1-57071-331-6	How to Negotiate Real Estate Contracts (3E)	$16.95
____	1-57071-332-4	How to Negotiate Real Estate Leases (3E)	$16.95
____	1-57071-225-5	How to Register Your Own Copyright (2E)	$19.95
____	1-57071-226-3	How to Register Your Own Trademark (2E)	$19.95
____	1-57071-349-9	How to Win Your Unemployment Compensation Claim	$19.95
____	1-57071-167-4	How to Write Your Own Living Will	$9.95
____	1-57071-344-8	How to Write Your Own Premarital Agreement (2E)	$19.95
____	1-57071-333-2	Jurors' Rights (2E)	$9.95
____	1-57248-032-7	Legal Malpractice & Other Claims ...	$18.95
____	1-57071-400-2	Legal Research Made Easy (2E)	$14.95
____	1-57071-336-7	Living Trusts and Simple Ways to Avoid Probate (2E)	$19.95

Qty	ISBN	Title	Retail
____	1-57071-345-6	Most Valuable Bus. Legal Forms You'll Ever Need (2E)	$19.95
____	1-57071-346-4	Most Valuable Corporate Forms You'll Ever Need (2E)	$24.95
____	1-57248-098-X	The Nanny and Domestic Help Legal Kit	$19.95
____	1-57248-089-0	Neighbor vs. Neighbor (2E)	$12.95
____	1-57071-348-0	The Power of Attorney Handbook (3E)	$19.95
____	1-57248-020-3	Simple Ways to Protect Yourself from Lawsuits	$24.95
____	1-57071-337-5	Social Security Benefits Handbook (2E)	$14.95
____	1-57071-163-1	Software Law (w/diskette)	$29.95
____	0-913825-86-7	Successful Real Estate Brokerage Mgmt.	$19.95
____	1-57071-399-5	Unmarried Parents' Rights	$19.95
____	1-57071-354-5	U.S.A. Immigration Guide (3E)	$19.95
____	0-913825-82-4	Victims' Rights	$12.95
____	1-57071-165-8	Winning Your Personal Injury Claim	$19.95
____	1-57248-097-1	Your Right to Child Custody, Support and Visitation	$19.95
	CALIFORNIA TITLES		
____	1-57071-360-X	CA Power of Attorney Handbook	$12.95
____	1-57071-355-3	How to File for Divorce in CA	$19.95
____	1-57071-356-1	How to Make a CA Will	$12.95
____	1-57071-357-X	How to Start a Business in CA	$16.95
____	1-57071-408-8	How to Probate an Estate in CA	$19.95
____	1-57071-358-8	How to Win in Small Claims Court in CA	$14.95
____	1-57071-359-6	Landlords' Rights and Duties in CA	$19.95
	FLORIDA TITLES		
____	1-57071-363-4	Florida Power of Attorney Handbook (2E)	$12.95
____	1-57248-093-9	How to File for Divorce in FL (6E)	$21.95
____	1-57248-086-6	How to Form a Limited Liability Co. in FL	$19.95
____	1-57071-401-0	How to Form a Partnership in FL	$19.95

Form Continued   **Subtotal**   ___

Qty	SBN	Title	Retail
		FLORIDA TITLES (CONT'D)	
_____	1-57071-361-8	How to Make a FL Will (5E)	$12.95
_____	1-57248-088-2	How to Modify Your FL Divorce Judgement (4E)	$22.95
_____	1-57071-380-4	How to Form a Corporation in FL (4E)	$19.95
_____	1-57071-380-4	How to Form a Limited Liability Company in FL	$19.95
_____	1-57071-380-4	How to Probate an Estate in FL (3E)	$24.95
_____	1-57248-081-5	How to Start a Business in FL (5E)	$16.95
_____	1-57071-362-6	How to Win in Small Claims Court in FL (6E)	$14.95
_____	1-57071-335-9	Landlords' Rights and Duties in FL (7E)	$19.95
_____	1-57071-334-0	Land Trusts in FL (5E)	$24.95
_____	0-913825-73-5	Women's Legal Rights in FL	$19.95
		GEORGIA TITLES	
_____	1-57071-376-6	How to File for Divorce in GA (3E)	$19.95
_____	1-57248-075-0	How to Make a GA Will (3E)	$12.95
_____	1-57248-076-9	How to Start Business in GA (3E)	$16.95
		ILLINOIS TITLES	
_____	1-57071-405-3	How to File for Divorce in IL (2E)	$19.95
_____	1-57071-415-0	How to Make an IL Will (2E)	$12.95
_____	1-57071-416-9	How to Start a Business in IL (2E)	$16.95
_____	1-57248-078-5	Landlords' Rights & Duties in IL	$19.95
		MASSACHUSETTS TITLES	
_____	1-57071-329-4	How to File for Divorce in MA (2E)	$19.95
_____	1-57248-108-0	How to Make a MA Will (2E)	$9.95
_____	1-57248-109-9	How to Probate an Estate in MA (2E)	$19.95
_____	1-57248-106-4	How to Start a Business in MA (2E)	$16.95
_____	1-57248-107-2	Landlords' Rights and Duties in MA (2E)	$19.95
		MICHIGAN TITLES	
_____	1-57071-409-6	How to File for Divorce in MI (2E)	$19.95
_____	1-57248-077-7	How to Make a MI Will (2E)	$12.95
_____	1-57071-407-X	How to Start a Business in M (2E)	$16.95
		MINNESOTA TITLES	
_____	1-57248-039-4	How to File for Divorce in MN	$19.95
_____	1-57248-040-8	How to Form a Simple Corporation in MN	$19.95
_____	1-57248-037-8	How to Make a MN Will	$9.95
_____	1-57248-038-6	How to Start a Business in MN	$16.95

Qty	SBN	Title	Retail
		NEW YORK TITLES	
_____	1-57071-184-4	How to File for Divorce in NY	$19.95
_____	1-57248-105-6	How to Form a Corporation in NY	$19.95
_____	1-57248-095-5	How to Make a NY Will (2E)	$12.95
_____	1-57071-185-2	How to Start a Business in NY	$16.95
_____	1-57071-187-9	How to Win in Small Claims Court in NY	$14.95
_____	1-57071-186-0	Landlords' Rights and Duties in NY	$19.95
_____	1-57071-188-7	New York Power of Attorney Handbook	$19.95
		NORTH CAROLINA TITLES	
_____	1-57071-326-X	How to File for Divorce in NC (2E)	$19.95
_____	1-57071-327-8	How to Make a NC Will (2E)	$12.95
_____	1-57248-096-3	How to Start a Business in NC (2E)	$16.95
_____	1-57248-091-2	Landlords' Rights & Duties in NC	$19.95
		OHIO TITLES	
_____	1-57248-102-1	How to File for Divorce in OH	$19.95
		PENNSYLVANIA TITLES	
_____	1-57071-177-1	How to File for Divorce in PA	$19.95
_____	1-57248-094-7	How to Make a PA Will (2E)	$12.95
_____	1-57248-112-9	How to Start a Business in PA (2E)	$16.95
_____	1-57071-179-8	Landlords' Rights and Duties in PA	$19.95
		TEXAS TITLES	
_____	1-57071-330-8	How to File for Divorce in TX (2E)	$19.95
_____	1-57248-009-2	How to Form a Simple Corporation in TX	$19.95
_____	1-57071-417-7	How to Make a TX Will (2E)	$12.95
_____	1-57071-418-5	How to Probate an Estate in TX (2E)	$19.95
_____	1-57071-365-0	How to Start a Business in TX (2E)	$16.95
_____	1-57248-111-0	How to Win in Small Claims Court in TX (2E)	$14.95
_____	1-57248-110-2	Landlords' Rights and Duties in TX (2E)	$19.95

SUBTOTAL THIS SIDE _____

SUBTOTAL OTHER SIDE _____

Illinois residents add 6.75% sales tax Florida residents
add 6% state sales tax plus applicable discretionary surtax _____

Shipping — $4.00 for 1st book, $1.00 each additional _____

TOTAL _____